A Strategy for Managing Water in the Middle East and North Africa

The World Bank
Washington, D.C.

© 1994 The International Bank for Reconstruction
and Development/THE WORLD BANK
1818 H Street, N.W.
Washington, D.C. 20433

All rights reserved
Manufactured in the United States of America
First printing July 1994

This report is a study by the World Bank's staff, and the judgments made herein
do not necessarily reflect the views of the Board of Executive Directors or of the
governments they represent. The boundaries, colors, denominations, and other
information shown on any map in this volume do not imply on the part of the
World Bank Group any judgment on the legal status of any territory or the
endorsement or acceptance of such boundaries.

The cover photograph shows a detail of a water fountain in Morocco.

This paper was prepared by Jeremy Berkoff, Senior Water Resources Economist,
Water Resources Management Unit, Technical Department, Europe and Central
Asia/Middle East and North Africa Regions. Extensive advice and assistance
were provided by Tariq Husain, David Howarth, John Hayward, Warren
Fairchild, Janusz Kindler, and Ulrich Kuffner. The paper was written in close
cooperation with MENA operations staff, from whom numerous helpful
comments and suggestions were received. It conforms to the Water Policy Paper
prepared by staff of the Environmentally Sustainable Development (ESD) Vice
Presidency and approved by the Board of the World Bank in May 1993.

Library of Congress Cataloging-in-Publication Data

Berkoff, Jeremy, 1943–
    A strategy for managing water in the Middle East and North Africa
    / Jeremy Berkoff.
        p.   cm. — (Directions in development)
    Includes bibliographical references (p.   ).
    ISBN 0-8213-2709-7
    1. Water resources development—Middle East. 2. Water resources
    development—Africa, North.   I. Title.   II. Series: Directions in
    development (Washington, D.C.)
    HD1698.M53B47   1994
    333.91'00956—dc20   93-23728
                                                               CIP

Contents

Foreword	*v*
Glossary	*vii*
Acronyms	*viii*
Map Freshwater Resources in the Middle East and North Africa	*x*
Summary	*xi*

1. Introduction   *1*
    The World Bank's Water Resources Program   *4*
    The World Bank's Policy Paper   *7*
    The MENA Strategy Paper   *8*

2. The Water Situation in MENA   *9*
    Long-Term Trends in Supply and Demand   *9*
    Water Quality and Environmental Issues   *13*
    International Waters   *15*

3. Managing Water in the MENA Region   *20*
    Water Resources Management and Planning   *20*
    Supply Management   *26*
    Demand Management   *31*
    Conclusions   *38*

4. Institutional Issues   *40*
    Legislation and Regulation   *41*
    Agency Functions and Organization   *42*
    Management of the Resource   *44*
    Delivery of Water Services   *47*
    Staff Capability and Training   *50*
    International Issues   *51*
    Conclusions   *52*

iv   CONTENTS

5. Water Strategies for the MENA Region *53*
  Strategies at the National Level *53*
  Strategies at the Sectoral level *55*
  World Bank Strategy at the National Level *60*
  World Bank Strategy at the International Level *62*
  Concluding Remarks *63*

Appendix Tables *65*
  Table A-1. Projects with Water as Primary Purpose,
   by Region, FY 1960–Mid-FY 1992 *65*
  Table A-2. Projects with Water as Primary Purpose in MENA,
   FY 1960–Mid-FY 1992 *66*
  Table A-3. Sector Studies and Memoranda with Water
   Components, MENA Region *67*
  Table A-4. Water Availability, MENA Region *68*
  Table A-5. Water Withdrawals, MENA Region *69*
  Table A-6. Irrigated Areas, MENA Region *70*

References *71*

Foreword

Water has always been of central concern to life in the Middle East and North Africa (MENA). Early civilizations emerged along the Tigris-Euphrates and Nile, and the struggle for water shaped life in desert communities. But concerns of the past are dwarfed by those of the present century. Burgeoning populations are placing unprecedented pressures on the resource, calling urgently for new approaches to water planning and management if escalating conflicts are to be avoided and if environmental degradation is to be reversed.

Since its inception, the World Bank has placed major emphasis on assisting countries to tackle their water resource problems. But emerging pressures, felt acutely in MENA and faced in varying degrees throughout the world, have led the Bank to reconsider the way it approaches water issues. The new Water Resources Management Policy, approved by the Board in May 1993, requires a shift in focus from the needs of individual water-using sectors to an integrated management approach. Water is to be explicitly treated as a key resource for economic and social development, with emphasis placed on managing water demands and water quality in the interests of the whole community.

This booklet sets out the implications of the new Bank policy for the MENA region, calling for a concerted effort by government and Bank staff to address water resources in a coordinated and sustainable manner. It proposes a practical, step-by-step approach to achieving this objective that could lead to new Bank-supported operations to address the water sector as a whole.

The issues involved in effective water resource management are complex and often politically sensitive. But they cannot be avoided if water scarcity is not to place undue costs on the whole development process. It is hoped that the strategy set out in this paper will contribute to *vi* FOREWORD

building a new partnership between the World Bank and MENA governments in sustainable water management and help the peoples of the region in their adjustment to a period of increasing water scarcity.

Caio Koch-Weser
Vice President
Middle East and North Africa Region

Glossary

Aquifer. An underground stratum capable of storing water and transmitting it to wells, springs, or surface water bodies.

Artesian. An aquifer that is under pressure.

Comprehensive water resources framework. An analytic framework for water resources management that views water as a single resource with many uses and interlinkages with the ecological and socioeconomic system.

Consumptive water use. Water withdrawn from a surface or groundwater body which, because of absorption, transpiration, evaporation, or incorporation in a manufactured product, is not returned directly to a supply source.

Demand management. Use of measures and practices including education and awareness programs, metering, water pricing, quantitative restrictions, and other devices, to manage and control the demand for water.

Depletion. The withdrawal of water from surface or groundwater water bodies at a rate greater than the rate of replenishment (recharge rate).

Drip irrigation. Localized drop-by-drop application of water that uses pipes, tubes, filters, emitters, and ancillary devices to deliver water to specific sites at a point or grid on the soil surface.

Externality. The side effect of one party's actions on another party or parties, including both the general public and specific entities.

Fossil aquifer. A term sometimes used to refer to large aquifers dating from the remote past. In practice, few such aquifers are true fossils since

vii

viii GLOSSARY

they continue to be recharged even though the recharge rate is typically very small relative to total storage.

Groundwater mining. The condition when withdrawals are made from an aquifer at rates in excess of net recharge.

Instream water use. Use of water which does not require withdrawal or diversion from its natural watercourse.

Interbasin transfer. The physical transfer of water from one drainage basin to another.

Market failure. A divergence between the (prevailing) market solution and the economically efficient solution.

Riparian state. A state through or along which a portion of a river flows or a lake lies.

Multipurpose development. Development of a particular water resource to serve two or more purposes simultaneously.

Recycling process. Withdrawal of water for use in cooling or processing and the subsequent reconditioning and repeated reuse of the same water, usually with relatively small additions of "makeup" water to compensate for losses through evaporation or otherwise.

River basin. The land area from which water drains into a river.

Runoff. That part of precipitation which appears in surface streams.

Storage. The impoundment of water in surface reservoirs or its accumulation in underground reservoirs.

Unaccounted-for-water. The difference between the volume of water delivered into a supply system and the volume of water accounted for by legitimate consumption, whether metered or not.

User charge. A charge to direct users of water for water withdrawal, instream use, or assimilation of waste.

Acronyms

AIC	Average incremental cost
BCM	Billion cubic meters
BOT	Build, operate, and transfer
CWA	Country water assessment
CWAS	Country water assessment and strategy
ESD	Environmentally sustainable development
IDA	International Development Association
MENA	Middle East and North Africa
METAP	Mediterranean environmental technical assistance program
MN1	Country Department I
MN2	Country Department II
MW	Megawatt
NWS	National water strategy
OED	Operations Evaluation Department
O&M	Operations and maintenance
POM	Plan of operations and maintenance
UNDP	United Nations Development Program
UNDTC	United Nations Department of Technical Cooperation
UNEP	United Nations Environmental Program
USDA	United States Department of Agriculture
WDR	World Development Report
WUA	Water User Association

Note

The World Bank's MENA Region comprises the following countries:

Country Department 1: Algeria, Iran, Libya, Malta, Morocco, Tunisia
Country Department 2: Bahrain, Egypt, Iraq, Jordan, Kuwait, Lebanon, Oman, Qatar, Saudi Arabia, Syria, United Arab Emirates, Yemen Republic

Eight countries are currently active borrowers from the Bank: Algeria, Egypt, Iran, Jordan, Lebanon, Morocco, Tunisia, and Yemen.

MENA REGION

FRESHWATER RESOURCES IN THE MIDDLE EAST AND NORTH AFRICA

Summary

The water situation in the Middle East and North Africa (MENA) is precarious. Population and development have overwhelmed traditional management practice, and problems of water scarcity and pollution are as severe as anywhere in the world. Within one lifetime (1960 to 2025) per capita renewable supplies will have fallen from 3,430 cubic meters to 667 cubic meters, and in several countries of the region renewable freshwater will barely cover basic human needs into the next century. Rivers and aquifers crossing national borders lead to conflicts and difficult issues of effective resource management.

If water is abundant, it can be used with little regard for impacts elsewhere. But as demands increase, as they have in MENA, cross-sectoral interactions and external effects mount. Management approaches that fail to account for these interactions can be very costly. Moreover, as the limits of economically renewable supplies are approached, difficult reallocation issues must be addressed if the impending crisis is to be effectively managed and if costly desalination and other nonconventional sources are to be avoided.

The Bank has been prominent in water development, and water projects have accounted for about 14 percent of lending worldwide and 16 percent in MENA. The region has been relatively advanced in tackling broader water resource issues. But, in common with other parts of the Bank, most activities have focused on specific sectors rather than on the resource, with a greater share going to water supply and sanitation, and a lesser share to irrigation, than in other regions. There have been surprisingly few multipurpose projects, and the focus on specific sectors has meant that some broader-based opportunities have been missed.

The urgency of water issues is increasingly recognized worldwide and there is growing consensus on the principles that should guide action in this area. This is recognized in a Bank policy paper (World Bank 1993), recently approved by the Bank's board, which requires Bank staff to focus on three main elements: first, that water should be viewed as a limited resource to be managed in an integrated manner to meet national objectives—economic, social, security, environmental—rather than as

xi

xii SUMMARY

an input into specific sectors; second, that institutional reform and capacity building are critical to sustaining policies, programs, and projects; and third, that international water issues should be given particular attention.

A Strategy for Managing Water in the Middle East and North Africa proposes a strategy that is consistent with the Bank's policy paper and aims to help governments and Bank staff address water resource issues in an integrated and sustainable manner. Given the region's specific conditions, and the technical and economic characteristics of water, it proposes practical approaches that seek to recognize both the complexity and the urgency of the water resources issues faced in the region.

Water Resources Management in MENA

Water resources management in the MENA region and the institutional arrangements needed to support management improvements must respond to the acute shortages in renewable water supplies and to growing pressures on the environment.

The Water Situation in MENA

Annual renewable resources in MENA average about 350 billion cubic meters (BCM) or 1,436 cubic meters/head, of which some 120 BCM are accounted for by river flows from outside the region. In 1990, of eighteen MENA countries only seven had per capita availability of more than 1,000 cubic meters/year and by 2025 the regional average is projected at no more than 667 cubic meters (30 percent of the Asia estimate, 25 percent of that for Africa, and 15 percent of that for the world). Not only is water scarce but rivers are highly variable and difficult to manage. Many countries are mining groundwater, a temporary and often risky expedient. The region also accounts for 60 percent of world desalination capacity but this option is only open to oil rich countries.

Irrigation accounts for some 80 percent of withdrawals regionwide but demand is expanding most rapidly in urban areas. The region is highly urbanized and the share of domestic and industrial demand in the total is already higher than in other parts of the developing world. By 2025, the share of population living in urban areas will increase from 60 percent to nearly 75 percent. Withdrawals in Libya, Saudi Arabia, the Gulf States, and Yemen already exceed renewable supplies while Egypt, Israel, and Jordan are essentially at the limit. Moreover, Algeria, Iran, Morocco, and Tunisia face severe regional deficits even if in total they are in surplus. Though water transfers are sometimes feasible, they can be very expensive, and full mobilization of surplus supplies is always impracticable. Only Iraq and Lebanon appear to have renewable supplies adequate relative to population and even these face major problems of adjustment.

Major water resources in the region are shared between countries lying both within and beyond the region. The most significant river basins are those of the Jordan, Nile, and Euphrates/Tigris, all of which are subject to contentious riparian issues. A significant agreement exists only in respect of the Nile, and then only between two countries (Egypt and Sudan). Large aquifers underlie North Africa and the Arabian Peninsula. Though costly to develop, they could be shared by several countries but agreement on abstractions will be difficult.

Deteriorating water quality is an increasingly serious issue in many areas due to a combination of low river flows, inadequate treatment, agricultural runoffs, and uncontrolled effluent from industry. Declining quality directly affects the utility of the resource, and treatment costs will rise steeply if rivers and potable aquifers are to be sustained in usable forms. Most health costs are associated with biological pollution although chemical pollutants from industry and intensive agriculture are increasingly damaging. Seawater intrusion into coastal aquifers is a critical issue in most locations, and waterlogging and secondary salinity affect several of the major irrigated areas.

Water Management and Water Planning

Water quantity and water quality are inseparable since all water uses require that water quality fall within a range specific to that use. Water management and planning must therefore deal appropriately with both aspects in an integrated fashion depending on prevailing circumstances. Management issues can conveniently be considered under two headings: supply management (activities required to locate, develop, and manage new sources) and demand management (mechanisms to promote more desirable levels and patterns of water use). Planning integrates these along with environmental concerns, and provides the analytical basis for choosing between alternatives.

The need for systematic planning reflects the unique characteristics of water, notably its variable and unitary nature and the need for government intervention in its management due to prevalent issues of market failure. But the meaning of "planning" in this context must be understood. It does not mean that government should control each and every aspect of resource management. Many important activities are preferably decentralized to autonomous local, private, or user entities. Nor does *xiv* SUMMARY

it mean that governments alone should be responsible for setting objectives and priorities. On the contrary, stakeholder participation in decisionmaking not only promotes accountability and transparency but also almost always leads to solutions that are more efficient and resilient.

Governments have typically emphasized *Supply Management* but as new water sources become increasingly inaccessible, the costs of projects to augment supply escalate. The potential for new storage and diversion projects in MENA is limited and political objections to interbasin water transfers may prove insurmountable even if the formidable financing and implementation problems could be overcome. Many countries are already dependent on groundwater and, despite potential for further exploitation (e.g., from costly deep aquifers), most countries face severe problems of depletion. Nonconventional sources include wastewater treatment and reuse, and desalination. They are invariably more expensive than traditional sources although in the case of wastewater treatment costs can be offset against environmental concerns. Alternatives to new investment are conservation and improved management of existing supplies, both of which are normally very cost effective. More problematic is reallocation between uses. Reallocation will be a key mechanism for adjusting to water scarcity since relatively small shifts from irrigation can often satisfy the needs of other sectors. But abandoning irrigation in arid areas destroys agricultural viability and has adverse multiplier and third-party effects. Increased efficiency should always be emphasized but few governments are willing to commit themselves to a strategy of reducing irrigated areas—or even to the use of (costly) treated wastewater in irrigation—even if they recognize that this is inevitable in the longer term.

Given the constraints on new supplies, governments must be persuaded to give far greater emphasis to *Demand Management*. Demand management covers both direct measures to control water use (e.g., regulation, technology), and indirect measures that affect voluntary behavior (e.g., market mechanisms, financial incentives, public education). The mix of demand management measures will vary but in all cases they aim to conserve water through the increased efficiency—and perhaps equity—of water use.

Direct measures to control water use are difficult to administer although rationing can be effective in response to variability, and regulation of water quality is a universal objective even if seldom successful. Technical interventions are important in all sectors to reduce unaccounted-for water and losses. Modernization of both distribution and onfarm systems has particular potential. Indirect measures notably include water charges and other financial instruments. In principle, opportunity cost pricing would provide appropriate incentives for efficient use of water and governments should be strongly encouraged to bring resource pricing progressively closer to real economic levels. In practice, even if water use is measured and fees are charged according to the volume of water used, rates usually fall below those required to cover financial costs, let alone have a significant impact on demand. Indeed, in some countries, irrigation is provided to the farmer free and in all countries there is strong resistance to effective water pricing. Markets can have some role in setting prices. For instance, local water markets invariably emerge where private interests control particular water supplies and should be actively facilitated. But allocation of supplies through market mechanisms over greater distances or between major sectors will be difficult to achieve, at least for the foreseeable future.

Institutional Issues

Institutions in their widest sense comprise organizations, laws, decrees, regulations, customs, markets, and all that are associated with these. They largely determine whether objectives can be achieved in practice. The transition from an emphasis on supply management to a balanced strategy for managing both water supply and demand must be complemented by institutional reform. Most institutional issues must be tackled at the national level. International treaties with respect to shared water resources will also be an essential precondition for optimizing their development and management.

Legislation provides the basis for government action in the regulatory and operational areas and establishes the context for action by private entities and individuals. In Islamic tradition, water is a gift from God and belongs to the community. Value-added gives a qualified right to appropriation but few water statutes establish clear allocation priorities. With growing scarcity, coherent legislation will become increasingly necessary if the high costs of *ad hoc* approaches to water allocation and control are to be avoided. Administrative weaknesses will inevitably constrain the effectiveness of legislation. Even so, enforcement of rights and standards will remain critical to resource management and the need to strengthen administrative efficiency cannot be avoided.

Government has dominated water services, typically through single purpose ministries and departments. But fragmented arrangements become increasingly inadequate in an environment of competing uses. Solutions are complex and country-specific but can usefully be considered in relation to: (i) management of the resource and (ii) delivery of water services:

- *Management of the Resource* embraces policy, allocation, and environmental aspects and is inherently a government function. This in no way precludes a crucial role for stakeholder participation in decisionmaking. Nor does it mean that all functions must be concentrated at the center. National policy and planning is intrinsically a centralized activity but many other aspects are preferably delegated to regional, basin, or local levels.
- *Delivery of Water Services* involves wholesaling of water to intermediaries and retail distribution to end users—farmers in an irrigation scheme, households in a municipality etc. It can be either by public or private entities but increased private participation should be actively pursued in view of the incentives private ownership and/or management has for supplying cost-effective and quality service. Whether in the private or the public sectors, delivery of services is usually best assigned to autonomous agencies (utilities) operating at a local level and delivering specified services to their customers for a fee.

To be successful, training and staff development in public agencies must be associated with motivating incentives. This is most readily achieved within the context of autonomous utilities and even more so in the private sector. It will be more difficult to achieve in agencies responsible for important resource planning and management functions. However, this is a further issue that cannot be avoided given the necessity for coherent planning and the complex resource problems faced in many MENA countries.

National, International, and Bank Water Strategies in MENA

Governments are primarily responsible for addressing water resource management issues at the national level, and governments in cooperation for joint action at the regional, subregional, or river-basin level. The Bank stands ready to support government and regional strategies and actions.

Strategies at the National Level

Arguments in favor of an integrated approach to water management are persuasive. Key considerations include the following: (1) water is a unitary resource requiring systematic planning to reflect its full economic value; (2) water quality should be considered simultaneously with water quantity; (3) data collection, processing, and dissemination are of critical importance; (4) policies for protecting natural water environments should be incorporated into water allocation principles and regulatory measures; (5) stakeholders at each level should fully participate in establishing objectives and priorities; (6) difficult issues of reallocation notably from irrigation cannot be avoided; (7) demand management should be given a central role involving both direct and indirect mechanisms; (8) high priority should be given to capacity building and institutional reform; (9) delivery of water services should to the extent possible be decentralized to autonomous utilities; (10) privatization of utility services should be promoted; and (11) agreements between riparian countries should provide the basis for water allocation and investment activities concerning international surface water, groundwater, and water quality.

Planning must be iterative, and there is no alternative to a permanent institutional capacity as a basis for sound decisionmaking. But preparation of a country water assessment (CWA) leading to a national water strategy (NWS) will often be a useful interim step to help clarify application of the principles set out above in a country context, and reach consensus among the many actors involved. The CWA would take stock of water problems and issues leading to a long-term strategy for water resources development and management. As such it would provide a framework for ensuring consistency at the sectoral level; ensure harmonization of water resources and environmental objectives; assess financing issues and requirements; and establish priorities for further analytical work.

The above should be complemented by water conservation measures within specific sectors, notably irrigation, with instream uses and reuse of treated wastewater given increased attention. Water savings from specific conservation measures will need careful hydrological analysis, as water "losses" from one project may be reused by others downstream. In most cases, however, conservation can be expected to have priority, especially where savings can be associated with increases in production as is often the case in irrigation. Conservation measures in irrigation include improved water scheduling and operations, modernization of irrigation networks and onfarm systems, use of less water-intensive crops, and complementary agricultural research. In municipalities and industry, conservation and reduction in the volume of wastewater treatment and disposal will become increasingly important. Policy reforms in setting water charges and wastewater disposal should be strongly supported. Location of new industries, including thermal power plants, should be dependent on the effects on the water resources, *xviii* SUMMARY

and appropriate remedial measures should be instituted for existing industries.

The natural potential for flash flood damage in the region has been much reduced by engineering works but there is a need to change the way countries perceive their flood problems. In general, the cumulative value of a river's flood pulse (nutrient supply to floodplain, natural floodwater irrigation, groundwater recharge, fisheries, etc.) has been underestimated. Long-term and sustainable economic interests may sometimes be better served by building on the floodpulse and flood dependent production systems (recessional agriculture, floodplain fisheries, and grazing) rather than suppressing them.

Strategies at the International Level

The predominance of international rivers and aquifers in the MENA region limits the extent to which water problems can be resolved at country level. But reaching agreement on international waters is a time-consuming, difficult, and complex process. Riparian countries should be strongly encouraged to participate in international resolution of water issues and governments should be made aware that the Bank stands ready to provide technical, legal, and intermediary support for such initiatives.

Strategies for the Bank

Bank staff need to establish and maintain consistent strategies to guide their work at the regional and country levels. With respect to individual countries, the country departments should review objectives on a country-by-country basis and schedule Bank activities to meet those objectives. With respect to international rivers and aquifers, the region should consider a more proactive role on a case-by-case basis.

Lending provides the Bank with the main context for pursuing a sector dialogue and lending instruments should be evolved to promote agreed objectives, an essential feature being integrated approaches to water resource management. Individual sectors will still involve issues that go beyond those associated with resource management. Typically, therefore, the Bank should envisage complementary lending at the level both of the resource (e.g., a water adjustment operation or support for a time slice of water investments) and of individual multipurpose projects and sectors. Some countries may be unsuited to a water resource management operation, or their governments may be unwilling to accept it. In such cases, lending at the level of an individual project or sector must still be designed to assure consistency with the overall country water strategy and be conditional on satisfactory progress in meeting general resource objectives.

Implications for the Bank's sector work and technical assistance are relatively straightforward. Priority should be given to preparation of country water assessments and strategy documents, and to the Bank's role in international water issues. The country strategy would schedule further detailed analytical work and technical assistance. Particular attention needs to be given to coordinating environmental sector and project work with that on water resources. Water often represents the critical environmental issue and it is crucial that environmental sector work reflects a realistic and practical appreciation of resource management issues. Similarly, issues of water quality are inherent to any water strategy, and CWAs and other water sector work must reflect environmental concerns in an integral manner.

1. Introduction

The water situation in MENA is precarious. Population growth and economic development have overwhelmed traditional water management practice and water scarcity and mounting pollution are faced to varying degrees throughout the region. Issues of efficiency, allocation, and water quality must be urgently addressed if the impending crisis is to be effectively managed. Within one lifetime, annual average per capita renewable supplies—excluding so-called "fossil" aquifers—will have fallen by about 80 percent, from 3,430 cubic meters per capita (in 1960) to 667 cubic meters (in 2025). These levels are well below the levels of other major regions of the world (figure 1). In several MENA countries, renewable freshwater will barely cover basic human needs into the next

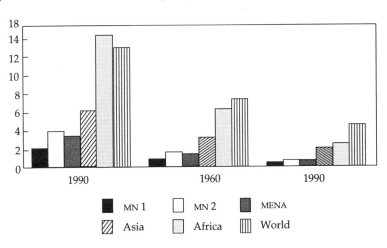

Figure 1. Renewable Resources by Major Region per Capita,

Note: Including net flows from other regions.
Source: World Resources Institute 1992.

century. Moreover, 35 percent of renewable supplies are provided by rivers flowing from outside the region and—to a varying extent—these are vulnerable to abstraction by upstream riparians. Within the region, rivers and aquifers crossing national borders can lead to acute conflicts and invariably involve complex issues of resource management. Two-thirds of all Arabic speaking peoples depend on rivers flowing from non-Arab countries, and almost 25 percent live in countries with essentially no perennial surface supplies. In all countries, the costs of pollution control will rise steeply, and expensive treated wastewater will have to provide an increasing source of supply.

The importance of water need not be belabored. It is essential to all life. In arid areas, it largely determines the pattern of settlement and plays a crucial role in human culture, religion, and history. Health and nutrition are dependent on water in adequate supplies of acceptable quality, and water is a key input for most economic activities. For millennia, civilization in the Middle East has depended on irrigated agriculture, and governments have almost invariably given irrigation high priority to feed rapidly growing populations. Fisheries, power,

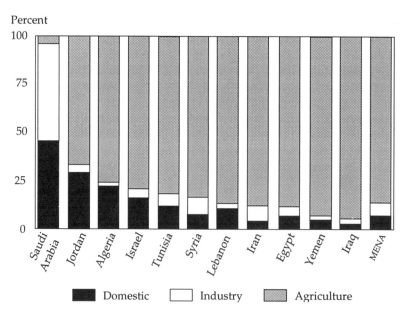

Figure 2. *Withdrawals by Major Sector in Selected MENA Countries*

Note: For various years, see appendix.
Source: World Resources Institute 1992.

transport, industry, and tourism are among other sectors in which water plays an important and often essential role. Other than in a few oil rich desert states, irrigation is by far the predominant user—accounting for more than 80 percent of withdrawals (figure 2)—though agriculture's share will decline rapidly with population growth and urbanization. These trends will also aggravate environmental and water quality problems. Already severe, such problems will worsen before they improve as documented in the 1992 World Development Report (WDR).

Table 1 indicates the level of investment in water resources for selected MENA countries in relation to GNP, public investment, and population. The totals include investments in the major water-using sectors, notably water supply and irrigation. No estimates are available for investment in raw water supply.

The table shows that water investments have been significant, typically accounting for between 10 and 20 percent of public sector investment, equivalent to perhaps 2 to 4 percent of GNP. Moreover, water components are included in a wide range of other programs and projects, which may not be fully reflected in these totals. Water is thus a major area of economic activity. It invariably has pervasive linkages to the national economy, and large scale water programs are often an essential basis for regional settlement and development activities.

Where water has been relatively abundant, individual sectors have developed and used surface and groundwater with little regard for impacts elsewhere. But as demands have increased, water quality has deteriorated and affected other users and the environment. Fragmented approaches that fail to take such externalities into account can be very costly. Moreover, as limits on economically available renewable water are approached, conservation and reallocation become increasingly the

Table 1. Water Resources Investment

		Water resources investment		
	GNP per capita 1985 dollars	*Percent of GNP*	*Percent of public investment*	*Dollars per capita*
Algeria	2,585	3.1	12.4	78.9
Jordan	1,111	3.7	16.0	41.1
Morocco	505	3.1	22.5	25.9
Tunisia	1,116	3.1	22.5	34.2
Yemen	562	1.9	n.a.	n.a.

n.a. = Not available.
Source: World Bank estimates.

only feasible alternatives to expensive desalination and other nontraditional sources. Conservation and reallocation are themselves sometimes costly and can involve difficult and complex political and institutional issues. And while Governments in MENA have given considerably more emphasis to water resource issues than those in most other parts of the world, the decisions required are politically difficult. Even so, the urgent nature of the issues faced requires that essential choices must be made if water is not to impose unnecessarily severe constraints on the whole development process.

World Bank's Water Resources Program

Since its beginnings, the Bank has been a key organization in fostering water resource development around the world. The Bank program has included loans and credits for water resources projects; extensive and varied economic and sector work; and technical assistance activities, including mediation in international disputes and its role as an executing agency for studies financed by the United Nations Development Programme (UNDP). Through its financing of water projects, the Bank has helped alleviate poverty, improve social well-being, and enhance environmental conditions in many countries.

The Lending Program

The magnitude of Bank involvement is illustrated by its lending program. From FY1960 through mid-FY1992, water projects made up about 14 percent of the lending program worldwide. The Board approved almost 800 projects involving water with Bank Group funding of about US$40 billion. During the same period, 100 projects involving water were approved in the MENA region with a commitment of almost US$4 billion. Approximately 16 percent of Bank Group lending in MENA has been in water. This is somewhat higher than for the Bank as a whole and reflects water scarcity in the region and its arid environment.

Bank lending in water worldwide has focused on irrigation, water supply and sanitation, hydropower, and—more recently—the environment. Irrigation has accounted for more than 50 percent of the total, and water supply and sanitation for a further 33 percent (appendix table A-1). Few projects are classified as multipurpose (15 out of almost 800) although several such projects have been implemented in the MENA region (e.g., Sidi-Salen in Tunisia) and sector-specific projects often form part of broader multipurpose programs. In MENA, the relative importance of the two main sectors—irrigation and water supply and sanitation—is reversed with the latter accounting for more than 50 percent of water lending (appendix table A-2 and figure 3). This reflects the acute water shortages faced in the region and the limited potential for expansion of irrigation. Only in Egypt has irrigation and drainage predominated in the Bank's program, reflecting the large investments in drainage infrastructure funded by the Bank as well as the substantial alternative sources of assistance for water supply and sanitation available to Egypt from the United States and other bilateral donors.

Performance of Bank Projects

The Bank's Operations Evaluation Department (OED) has filed more than 700 completion and audit reports on Bank-assisted water resources projects worldwide since 1972, as well as several review reports (OED 1981, OED 1991, OED 1992). More than 80 percent of these projects were judged to have performed satisfactorily, that is, remained economically viable and achieved project objectives. Nevertheless problems noted included the following:

Figure 3. Water Resource Management Strategy; Lending for Water as a Percentage of Total, FY 1960–FY Mid-1990

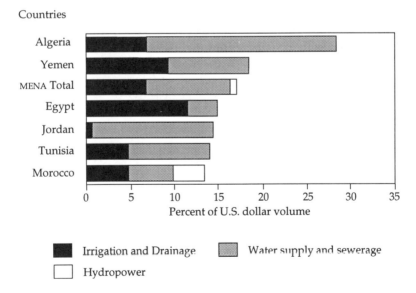

Source: Adapted from World Bank data base.

6 A STRATEGY FOR MANAGING WATER IN THE MENA REGION

- Most Bank efforts are sector-specific even where some issues are cross-sectoral
- Lending conditions relating to user charges are rarely met in full and borrowers remain generally uncommitted to financial sustainability
- More attention needs to be given to pricing and demand management issues
- Poor maintenance often threatens the physical sustainability of projects
- Efficiency and operational viability need to be addressed in greater depth
- Drainage and wastewater treatment have been given insufficient priority
- The potential of user groups and the private sector has been insufficiently exploited
- Public participation and stakeholder involvement in policy formulation and program development need much more attention.

A detailed review for this paper of OED results in four countries (Egypt, Tunisia, Algeria, and Morocco) confirms that these problems are also commonly encountered in MENA. In addition, this review pointed to the crucial role played in the success of specific projects by the early recognition of emerging water scarcity. Where investments reflected an early government response, the rate of success was relatively high (e.g., in Tunisia, which has a long history of water resources planning including that associated with the Bank-supported Sidi-Salen project). Where appreciation of such problems was lower—as for instance in Egypt—projects tend to be piecemeal, contributing to performance problems and failures in meeting technical or economic objectives.

Sector Work

Appendix table A-3 lists sector reports and studies completed in the MENA region. Most have been sector-specific but some recent reviews have taken a broader perspective, most notably the water sector studies undertaken in Jordan in 1984 and 1988 which built on earlier work undertaken in the context of the aborted Maqarin (Unity Dam) multipurpose project. Several recently initiated activities have also had a water resource focus (e.g., in Morocco, Lebanon, and Yemen). Despite their limited coverage, most sector-specific reviews have had a positive impact on sector policy and Bank lending. But sector-specific studies cannot properly address weaknesses in the broader context, and such studies themselves would often be more effective if set within a consistent overall framework.

Besides its own sector studies, the Bank acts as executing agency for UNDP-financed water sector planning studies (e.g., in Egypt) and coordinates its activities with those sponsored by other agencies (e.g., in Yemen) or the Government concerned (e.g., in Tunisia and Morocco). Water issues have also been included within the scope of environmental reviews and action plans. The first action plan was undertaken with the Government of Tunisia in 1988 and this has been followed by similar exercises in Egypt and other countries. Under the Mediterranean Environmental Technical Assistance Program (METAP), the Bank and other donor agencies have sponsored a range of studies with direct relevance to the region. These include two papers prepared in support of this paper (Coopers and Lybrand 1993; Frederick 1993).

Bank staff in the MENA region have been more advanced than in other regions of the Bank in tackling broader water resource issues, not only in the context of lending but also within the scope of sector work and environmental reviews. Even so, as in other parts of the Bank, most activities have focused on individual sectors. While many of these have been successful on their own terms, they would often have been enhanced if undertaken within the framework of coherent strategies for the exploitation and management of the overall resource, and opportunities for promoting such coherent strategies may have been missed.

The World Bank's Policy Paper

The urgency of water resource issues is gaining increasing recognition worldwide and there is a growing consensus on the principles that should guide action in this area. This consensus was expressed in the Dublin Statement issued at a preparatory meeting for the Earth Conference and endorsed at the main conference in Rio de Janeiro in May 1992 (UNEP 1992). In support of this approach, a Bank policy paper has been prepared and approved by the World Bank board (World Bank 1993a). Key elements are that the Bank adopt an integrated approach to water resource issues so as to account for the full economic costs of meeting national objectives. The paper proposes several conditions as a basis for the Bank's involvement:

- All water resource activities within a country—whether at the level of the resource or an individual sector—should reflect an explicit understanding with the government on a coherent approach to water resources management

- All such activities should, among others, address: (1) the adequacy of the data base; (2) both water quantity and water quality issues; (3) the economic and financial policy framework; (4) the legislative and regulatory framework; (5) institutional issues; and (6) stakeholder participation
- Water resources investments and policy reforms should be based on coherent water sector strategies at the regional, national, and international levels
- Sector specific water resource activities should include an assessment of the effects on other users and the environment
- The Bank should seek a more proactive role in international river issues, with development assistance predicated on a consensus by riparians with respect to both surface water and groundwater resources.

The Bank is preparing a guide to assist governments in formulating water resource strategies at the national level. A draft has been completed (World Bank 1993b), and once finalized this could make an important contribution to the implementation of the approach of the policy paper. Preparation of a country water assessment (CWA) leading to a national water strategy (NWS) is recommended below as a basis for preparing a coherent approach to water resource management at the country level (United Nations 1991).[1]

The MENA Strategy Paper

The main objective of this paper is to propose a strategy for the MENA region which is consistent with the Bank's policy paper and which can help governments and Bank staff address water resources in an integrated and sustainable manner. To this end, chapter 2 provides a brief overview of water resources in the region; chapter 3 suggests how countries might approach the management of water; chapter 4 presents ideas on the enabling institutional conditions; and chapter 5 reviews implementation issues. Internal procedures are concurrently being revised to strengthen the role of Bank staff in this process.

Note

1. Preparation of a "Country Water Assessment" (CWA) and water strategy was suggested at a UNDP-supported meeting held in Delft (United Nations 1991).

2. The Water Situation in MENA

Long-Term Trends in Supply and Demand

Supplies of renewable water are by definition limited whereas demand is rising rapidly in most countries. The implied imbalances can be anticipated in a planned and controlled manner. If not, the result may be arbitrary and chaotic reductions in demand as users compete for the limited supplies available.

Water Supplies

Annual renewable water resources in MENA average about 350 BCM (World Resources Institute 1992). Of this, about 120 BCM—or 35 percent—are provided by river flows from outside the region: 56 BCM by the Nile, 28 BCM by the Euphrates, and 38 BCM by the Tigris and its tributaries. Besides renewable surface water and groundwater, there are substantial nonrenewable groundwater resources, and countries in the region have varying access to brackish water and unlimited seawater. Appendix table A-4 compares renewable water resources per capita in MENA countries with estimates for other regions of the world. In 1990, only six MENA countries had per capita supply of more than 1,000 cubic meters per year. For MENA as a whole, per capita supply in 2025 is projected at 667 cubic meters per year, equivalent to only 30 percent of a comparable estimate for Asia, 25 percent of that for Africa, and 15 percent of that for the whole world. Perhaps the most striking aspect of these figures is the rapidity with which scarcity has arisen. In one lifetime, supply per capita will have fallen by over 80 percent, from 3,430 cubic meters in 1960 to 667 cubic meters in 2025 because of population growth.

Many countries—Algeria, Saudi Arabia, the Gulf States, Jordan, Israel, Yemen—mine groundwater. This may be a justified use of nonrenewable resources but cannot continue indefinitely. Mining of accessible groundwater resources is also often risky since interactions with river flows may affect surface supplies, and declining watertables can

10 A STRATEGY FOR MANAGING WATER IN THE MENA REGION

result in saline intrusion from brackish water or the sea. Mining of the nonrenewable supplies of the large, so-called fossil aquifers[1] is potentially longer term given the enormous volumes of water involved—the Nubian aquifer alone is estimated to contain more than 6,000 BCM or 20 times the average annual renewable supply for the region. Given their size, constraints on exploitation of these aquifers will ultimately be economic rather than physical. Not only are they often at great depth, but pumping costs will rise as watertables decline.

Nonconventional sources will become increasingly important. The region already accounts for about 60 percent of total world desalination capacity. Given its high cost (perhaps US$1.0–1.5 per cubic meters),[2] desalination is almost wholly confined to supplying industrial and domestic users in rich countries, with larger plants invariably associated with available cheap energy. Cost will be the constraint, in particular for inland cities. Similar considerations apply to water imports. For these, high cost is compounded by political issues associated with transfers across national boundaries. Within the region, wastewater will play an increasing role. Treatment and collection typically cost more than three times the cost of supply but these costs will be unavoidable not only to augment supply but also to ensure continued viability of sources threatened by pollution.

Variability in Supply

A major factor affecting water availability and pollution problems in MENA is its high seasonal and interannual variability. Annual precipitation varies from negligible amounts in desert areas to more than 1,500 mm in some mountainous regions with most rain falling in the winter months. Areas of moderate rainfall (500–750 mm) include Lebanon and northern Israel, most of northern and western Iran and the Maghreb as far inland as the southern slopes of the Atlas mountains. Streamflow varies markedly during the year in response to rainfall/run off patterns. Discharges in the low flow summer season typically average from one-fifth to one-tenth of the high flow winter season. Interannual variations are also greater in arid than in humid areas of the world. Water availability therefore fluctuates markedly about the averages in appendix table A-4. For example, low flows on the Tigris and Euphrates have been recorded at less than one third of the average annual flows and on the Jordan at less than one half.

Variability has three important implications for water management. First, it introduces an element of risk, which makes estimation of water's true opportunity cost—its value in the next best economic use—quite difficult. This is of particular relevance in MENA since the cross-sectoral comparison of water's opportunity cost becomes increasingly important as scarcity increases. Second, expensive storage capacity is required to utilize seasonal and interannual flows (though reservoirs in the region are also associated with high evaporation losses—for instance 14 percent of the Nile flow at Aswan is lost to evaporation from the reservoir). Groundwater storage could potentially play an increasingly important role in minimizing evaporation losses, but to date recharge in a planned manner is confined to a few locations (e.g., Israel, Jordan). Third, variability requires systematic contingency planning to ensure that responses to drought and—less commonly in the region—floods minimize adverse effects. Even within the range of normal variability, systematic responses are invariably required to distribute risk between different users in a planned and equitable manner.

Water Demands

Appendix table A-5 summarizes withdrawals by sector.[3] These estimates are taken from the publication "World Resources 1992–93." Other sources give substantially different estimates and the figures quoted must therefore be regarded as approximate. They may, for instance, understate withdrawals by industrial users which often have unrecorded captive sources of supply. In water-short regions the timing of withdrawals can also be important: for instance, large withdrawals over a short time period can critically affect both quality and instream uses.

The minimum water required to sustain human life is about 25 liters per day (say 10 cubic meters per year). A reasonable supply to maintain health may be 100–200 liters per day per capita (40–80 cubic meters per year) although in developed countries domestic use can exceed 300–400 liters per day (up to 150 cubic meters per year or more). By 2025—if fully mobilized—renewable resources in five MENA countries will barely cover basic human needs: Jordan, Libya, Malta, Saudi Arabia, and Yemen. Elsewhere, renewable supply would still exceed basic human requirements by varying—and in most cases considerable—amounts. However, not all renewable supplies can be mobilized at acceptable cost given their location and variability. The volume of economically available water is thus much lower than the estimates given in appendix table A-4.

With a few exceptions—Bahrain, Malta, Qatar, and Saudi Arabia—irrigation is by far the largest user, accounting for perhaps 85 percent of total use regionwide. Appendix table A-6 provides data on irrigated areas.

Between 1970 and 1987, the total irrigated area increased by about 2.5 million hectares or 15 percent, reaching 18.9 M ha. About 60 percent of this total is accounted for by four countries: Morocco, Egypt, Iraq, and Iran. Several countries, including Egypt, Morocco, and Syria, have plans for further major expansion. In the light of competing claims for scarce water resources, it is questionable whether these plans are realistic.

Though water use is predominantly in irrigation, demand for water is expanding most rapidly in urban areas. The region is already highly urbanized and the share of domestic and industrial demand is significantly higher than in other parts of the developing world. Most countries in the region are classified as middle income and the percentage of the urban population that has access to safe drinking water is approaching 100 percent. Urban sanitation coverage is also relatively high. In contrast, rural areas are much less well served, with only about 66 percent of the population having safe access. Population growth rates are expected to slow from about 3.0 percent between 1965 and 1990 to 2.4 percent between 1990 and 2030. Nevertheless, this rate of growth is still high by world standards and it is expected that total population would increase from about 245 million in 1990 to 525 million in 2025. The proportion living in urban areas is projected to increase from 60 percent to about 75 percent. The share of renewable water supplies absorbed in urban areas will thus need to rise from less than 10 percent to more than 20 percent simply to maintain present overall use rates. Increased efficiency in irrigation and reallocation from irrigation to other uses could in most countries provide sufficient renewable water to meet demands elsewhere. But reallocation from irrigation raises very difficult questions and, despite the costs involved, most countries continue to invest in expensive new supplies while maintaining allocations to relatively low-return agriculture.

The Water Balance

Only Iraq and Lebanon have renewable water resources that are adequate and well distributed relative to population. Even for these two countries, however, reservations are necessary. Iraq faces sharp reductions due to upstream development on the Euphrates and, to a lesser extent, the Tigris even if low flows might be improved through storage regulation. While it will remain well endowed by the—admittedly stringent—standards of the region, this will still force major adjustments in the way it manages its water and could have serious consequences in its delta areas. Lebanon must also tackle difficult management issues following the prolonged civil war. Moreover, in theory, diversion of its current surplus could contribute to resolving acute problems in neighboring countries even if, in practice, this may be unacceptable.

At the other extreme, withdrawals in several countries already exceed renewable supplies: Libya, Saudi Arabia, the Gulf States, Yemen. Others appear to be essentially at the limit or soon will be: Egypt, Israel, Jordan (although Appendix table A-4 understates the pressures faced in Jordan, since full Yarmouk flows appear to be included even though these are not fully available to Jordan, and overstates those in Egypt where return flows are inadequately accounted for). Algeria, Iran, Morocco, and Tunisia face severe regional deficits even if overall they are in surplus. Mobilizing local surpluses for use elsewhere is usually very expensive because of the transfer costs, and full mobilization is almost always impracticable due to resistance by present users and physical constraints.

Projecting water balances is an uncertain exercise as neither supply nor demand are quite what they seem. Beforehand, each sector can no doubt project its demands and the investment needed to meet these demands: if investment is limited by physical or financial constraints, then a deficit results. Ultimately, however, as for any commodity, supply and demand by definition balance. The question is whether this balance is to be achieved in a planned or unplanned manner, and at relatively high cost or relatively low cost. Since unlimited desalinated water can in principle be provided, the question is ultimately economic: can water be produced and used and wastes safely disposed of at costs justified by the value of the outputs produced? Put like this, the issue is susceptible to rational analysis. But attitudes to water are seldom straightforward, and the magnitude of the costs incurred and the conflicts so often involved mean that rational outcomes can be extremely difficult to attain.

Water Quality and Environmental Issues

Besides its role as a basic need and an economic input into productive sectors, water is also an environmental medium vital to human health and well-being. Comprehensive data on water quality in MENA are not available, but recent World Bank studies suggest that deteriorating water quality is becoming a serious issue in many countries. Although reliable comparative information is not available, numerous examples of emerging water quality problems are quoted in these papers. The principal sources of pollution include the following:

14 A STRATEGY FOR MANAGING WATER IN THE MENA REGION

- Untreated municipal wastewater, leaching from poorly maintained and functioning latrines and cesspools, and washing of fecal matter and other waste from the surface of the ground into water bodies
- Untreated industrial waste, discharging into municipal sewer systems or directly into water bodies
- Seepage from unsanitary landfills where the majority of the region's solid waste is dumped
- Seepage and runoff of agrochemicals such as fertilizers and non-biodegradable pesticides.

Declining water quality caused by contamination from these sources is affecting public health, the productivity of resources, and the quality of life. Once contaminated, groundwater seldom regenerates and, although rivers are to some extent self-cleansing, declining quality increases treatment costs to downstream users and may preclude reuse for particular purposes. Seawater intrusion into coastal aquifers is a critical issue in several countries—Libya, Israel, the Gulf States—and waterlogging and associated secondary salinity are widespread problems in many major irrigated areas (e.g., the Nile Delta, Upper Egypt, Iraq).

Public Health Risks

The first and most important impact of this trend is on public health. While infant mortality has declined significantly in the region, it remains well above world levels. The group most vulnerable to disease and illness related to poor quality water is children between birth and 14 years of age who account for over 43 percent of the region's population (a rate second only to sub-Saharan Africa). Five of the six leading causes of disease are waterborne. Waterborne diseases—especially diarrheal diseases—are second only to respiratory diseases in causing mortality and morbidity among this 0-to-14 age group. While many factors contribute to the spread of waterborne diseases, the combined experience during the recent UNDP Water Decade in both urban and rural areas has shown that their incidence could be reduced by over one-third by increasing the availability of uncontaminated water supplies. Improved sanitation, particularly increased household connection to sewers, could increase the impact by a further 20 percent.

Environmental Costs

The costs of providing water of appropriate quality is growing faster than the capacity to mobilize funds. The cost of water suitable for a particular use, already expensive because of the need to develop more marginal and distant sources, will increase further because of the added cost of treatment of raw water supplies and the cost of safe disposal of waste waters. Since water prices are typically well below the costs of providing supplies, there is no real incentive to recycle or minimize water use or waste generation. Low-cost water results in foregone revenue. Not only does this lead to underfunded operations and maintenance (O&M)—and consequently to poor performance and service—but it also limits the ability of local water organizations and the government to mobilize the investment funds required to satisfy today's and tomorrow's needs. In the Eastern Mediterranean, for example, funds will be needed between now and the year 2000 to provide about 120 million people, who are currently not served with safe water, in addition to the expected increase of about 130 million people over the same period. Expanded sanitation coverage will be needed for an even greater number of people because of the current low coverage. At a minimum of US$100–200 per capita for water and US$300–400 per capita for sewerage, this could imply total investment needs of up to US$125 billion or more.

Moreover, economically valuable resources are being lost. The potential of several countries, including Lebanon and Jordan, is predominantly as service-based economies. However, service activities are unlikely to locate in these countries if the environment is polluted and the infrastructure inadequate. Tourism in particular is one of the region's fastest growing industries, in 1989 providing up to 20 percent of the foreign exchange earnings of Jordan, Morocco, and Tunisia, and more than 10 percent of those of Egypt. Continued growth depends on the quality of tourist areas, which in many cases are threatened by water quality degradation. There are numerous examples of this problem, including many valuable beaches in Algeria, Tunisia, and—outside the region—Cyprus that are periodically closed to swimming and water sports—in some cases for years at a time—due to bacterial and other contamination caused by discharge of untreated municipal wastewater. Without effective monitoring and regulatory authorities capable of management and enforcement, problems can quickly grow to the point where they are unacceptably costly to rectify.

International Waters

Major water resources in the region are shared between countries. The three most important—and contentious—river basins are those of the Jordan, Nile, and Euphrates/Tigris. While the Jordan basin is entirely

16   A STRATEGY FOR MANAGING WATER IN THE MENA REGION

within the MENA region, both the Nile and the Euphrates/Tigris receive most of their flows from outside the region. Besides river flows, major aquifers also cross national boundaries.

The Jordan Basin

The Upper Jordan and its tributaries originate in Syria, Israel, and Lebanon. Jordan and the West Bank also have vested interests in Jordan river flows. The Upper Jordan is fed by springs with a relatively steady flow, the largest of which is the Dan Spring in Israel. The Hasbani River (northern tributary) is fed by springs in Lebanon. The Banias River is fed by the Hermon Spring in the Golan Heights in Syria. The Upper Jordan discharges its flow into Lake Tiberias which is the major storage within the basin. Israel diverts water directly from the lake into the National Water Carrier. The main tributary is the Yarmouk which flows between Syria and Jordan for about 40 kilometers before joining the Jordan 10 kilometers downstream of Lake Tiberias. Syria and Jordan withdraw water from the Yarmouk river to irrigate about 15,000 hectares and 12,000 hectares respectively (Jordan withdraws water via its main irrigation project, the East Ghor Canal). Below the confluence of the Jordan and Yarmouk rivers, springs and irrigation return flows contribute to the Jordan River before it discharges into the Dead Sea. This flow is heavily polluted by uses on both banks, an impact that is aggravated by the large-scale diversion of water by Israel out of the basin before it reaches the lower Jordan valley. The main issues are the conflicting claims of the riparian countries; the salinity and heavy pollution of the main Jordan river; the high population growth in Israel and Jordan; and the high rates of water use in both Israel and Jordan that exceed—or soon will exceed—renewable water resources in both countries.

The Nile Basin

The Nile is the dominant source of water for Egypt, the only MENA country in the Nile basin. Measured at Aswan, about 85 percent of average annual discharge originates from the Ethiopian highlands with most of the balance originating in Central Africa. To secure its water supply, Egypt has sought to enter into agreements with the upstream riparian countries, but has concluded agreements only with Sudan. A treaty was signed in 1959 between the two countries that specified their annual water shares. Since evaporation from the surface of Aswan Reservoir is substantial (about 14 percent of average flow), provision was made for sharing losses and gains equally by the two countries through joint water development projects. As the two governments agreed to share the total flow of the Nile, the treaty specifies that claims from other riparians would be jointly considered. If this meant an allotment to another country, the amount would be deducted from the shares of Egypt and Sudan in equal amounts. Ethiopia has never recognized the 1959 agreement and has declared that it violates its interests despite allowance in the Egypt-Sudan agreement for subsequent agreements with other riparian countries. The opposing views of Egypt, Sudan, and Ethiopia have been clearly stated at several conferences and meetings. Recently, however, the situation appears to be more promising. Technical contacts between the Nile basin countries are developing and awareness appears to be growing that the riparian nations must cooperate in the development, management, and conservation of the limited water resources available in the basin.

The Tigris and Euphrates Basins

The Euphrates originates in Turkey, which contributes 94 percent of the flow, 4 percent being added in Syria and no significant amount originating in Iraq. The Tigris receives about 40 percent of its flow from Turkey, 50 percent from Iraq, and 10 percent from Iran. The two rivers join to form the Shatt-al-Arab waterway before entering the Persian Gulf. Withdrawal for irrigation is the predominant water use in both basins, accounting for more than 80 percent of total abstractions. More than one million ha are irrigated in Iraq from the Euphrates, and more than two million ha from the Tigris and its tributaries. Although Syria and Turkey have much less irrigation, both have ambitious reclamation programs, and a significant proportion of the flow could be lost via evaporation from existing and proposed storage reservoirs. As cities grow and modernize, per capita consumption of water is also increasing. Projections show substantial depletion of water resources, especially in the Euphrates. While the Tigris is thought to have more water and to be less susceptible to depletions, it would also be substantially affected by the full development of all proposed irrigation projects, and in any case the two river systems are increasingly interconnected. These developments could lead to severe flow reductions in the Shatt-al-Arab, resulting in a deterioration of the situation in the lower reach of the river system and the delta. The main issue is thus reconciliation of conflicting interests of all the riparian countries.

International Aquifers

Several very large aquifers underlie MENA countries in North Africa and the Arabian Peninsula. Some of these cross national borders and are therefore claimed by neighboring countries. The most important of these disputed aquifers are the Eastern Erg, the Nubian, and the Saq/Disi. The Eastern Erg is located south of the Atlas mountains in Algeria and extends into Tunisia (see map on page *x*). It covers an area of almost 400,000 square kilometers and is artesian over most of this area. The volume of water stored is about four times the average annual renewable supply of the entire MENA region although only 0.04 percent of this volume is recharged annually. The Nubian Sandstone Aquifer underlies parts of Egypt, Libya, and Sudan, extending over an area of 1.8 million square kilometers of which about 150,000 square kilometers are under artesian conditions. The volume of stored water is nearly twenty times the average annual renewable supply for the MENA region, and the aquifer is fairly well recharged with annual recharge rate equal to about 2.5 percent of its volume. The most contentious issue is massive exploitation in southeastern Libya and the transfer of water to the Libyan coastal region via the so-called man-made river project. There is a fear that this may reduce substantially the groundwater reserves in the two other riparian countries. The Saq Formation (Disi Aquifer in Jordan) covers an area of 106,000 square kilometers and extends from Jordan to the east and south into Saudi Arabia. It is considered to be the best groundwater resource in Saudi Arabia. Jordan is concerned that the ongoing exploitation of the aquifer in Saudi Arabia for low-return wheat cultivation will reduce availability for higher priority uses and harm Jordanian interests. Jordan itself has also exploited the aquifer for agricultural purposes but currently envisages devoting it to urban and industrial uses.

The nature of these large aquifers requires extensive investigation to determine their characteristics, possible exploitation rates and the potential impacts on neighboring countries. Generally, however, they are characterized by shallow gradients and low permeability. Water levels and volumes are therefore not quickly affected over large distances. Pumping can, however, lead to a rapid decline in local watertables and to the exhaustion of a specific well or well field. Exploitation close to a border can thus still damage the interests of the neighboring country, and cooperative management and exploitation would undoubtedly provide the basis for the most equitable solution to disputes.

Notes

1. These aquifers almost invariably continue to receive some recharge although such recharge is very small relative to the volume of supply. Strictly speaking, therefore, they are not 'fossil' aquifers.

2. There are indications that average costs of desalination plants are declining and that desalination will become a more competitive source of supply, in particular for coastal cities.

3. Water withdrawn is water diverted from its natural course. Some part—often a large part—can usually be reused although not always near the point where the first withdrawal takes place.

3. Managing Water in the MENA Region

The urgency of addressing water issues is being increasingly recognized by MENA governments, and policy and institutional reforms are being considered in most countries. The Bank has contributed to the debate through a wide range of sector and project activities, and in recent years has been actively involved in water projects in Egypt, Algeria, Jordan, Morocco, Tunisia, and Yemen. However, fragmented approaches continue to weaken the effectiveness of most reform measures, and in most countries the urgency of these issues has yet to be adequately recognized in practical terms at the highest levels of government.

Policy and institutional reform in water is a complex process, and the full range of issues involved goes beyond the scope of this paper. However, some consideration of the more important issues is necessary as an introduction to the strategies proposed for the governments of MENA countries and the Bank in chapter 5. Chapter 3 therefore provides an overview of policy alternatives facing governments in the region, and chapter 4 discusses institutional issues that may need to be considered to sustain policy implementation.

Water Resources Management and Planning

Water resource management can be conveniently considered under two headings: *supply management*, which covers those activities required to locate, develop, and exploit new sources, and *demand management*, which addresses mechanisms to promote more desirable levels and patterns of water use.[1] *Planning* integrates the two aspects and provides the analytical basis for choosing between alternatives.

Managing Water Quantity and Water Quality

All water uses require that water quality falls within a range specific to that use. When water quality is outside this range—as when, for example, salinity is above the tolerance of crops, or contamination makes water unsuitable for industrial processes, or the level of biological or other contamination renders it unsafe for drinking or swimming—then the user must identify and develop an alternate source or reduce contamination to acceptable levels. These conditions impose large costs on water users. If there are no practical or economic treatment technologies, or if costs are greater than users can afford, then economic activities such as tourism, agriculture, or industry may be forced to move or cease operations.

Issues of quantity and quality are thus inseparable. If water is abundant relative to demand, quantity of supply raises no contentious issues. If water is abundant relative to levels of contamination, then quality is generally not an issue. Under such favorable circumstances, projects can be implemented that satisfy "needs" or targets in each sector—per capita consumption, industrial process demands, crop water requirements—without reference to the interests of others: sector, basin and project analysis can ensure selection of the most economic or least-cost alternatives to meet these targets; real-time operations can distribute supplies in response to day-to-day conditions; and maintenance in its broadest sense will determine whether the service intended—target allocations, assumed efficiencies, quality standards—can be sustained.

But as water scarcity grows, investment options diminish and contaminants are concentrated. Both the marginal costs of new supplies and the costs of dilution or removal of pollutants rise markedly. Not only are the best sites exploited first, but opportunity costs rise due to mounting externalities and foregone development in other uses. In a free market, the price would rise; water would shift from low-value to high-value uses; and incentives would be provided for efficient use and the preservation of water quality. However, market mechanisms are particularly problematic in water (box 1). No doubt local water markets often operate successfully. But it is unrealistic to expect that a general reallocation between sectors or improvements in water quality can be effected through the market, at least for the foreseeable future.[2] Governments must therefore assume ultimate responsibility for reallocation and preservation of environmental standards. Mechanisms include investment and allocation policy[3] (supply management), and measures that influence user behavior through direct regulation, technical innovation, financial incentive, or appeals for voluntary restraint (demand management). As shortages grow, the balance almost invariably—and often quite rapidly—must shift from development of new supplies towards modifications in allocation policy, water treatment, and demand management.

Water Resources Planning

Goals and objectives are set by government on behalf of their peoples, being evolved either autocratically or as a result of democratic processes that elicit participation of stakeholders in decisionmaking. Goals and objectives can be expressed in political, social, economic, or environmental terms. The planner's role is to evaluate the effects of alternative strategies on a consistent basis and to suggest policies and actions that can best achieve desired objectives. Thus, in its broadest sense, water resources planning provides the analytical basis for all policy formulation and for linking water resources issues to policies at the macroeconomic, regional, and sectoral levels.

The basic concepts that underlie water management are well documented (Rogers 1992) Some of the more important are summarized in

---

Box 1. Some Basic Concepts in Water Management

Water as a Unitary Resource. The natural hydrological unit comprises the interconnected surface and groundwater resources of a river basin or neighboring basins. Within this unit, management must be approached on a comprehensive basis to account for externalities. So long as water is abundant and of good quality, interactions are few and water projects can be implemented with little regard to their impact elsewhere. But as pressures mount, activities increasingly interact. Users compete for the same resource and water quality is modified in ways that affect its value to other users. Fragmented approaches that fail to account for these externalities can incur rapidly rising real costs.

Water as an Economic Good. Within the hydrological unit, renewable freshwater is a limited if variable resource. But in a broader sense, water is unlimited since freshwater can be imported from surplus areas and seawater can be desalinated and transported in any quantity at a price. Beyond the basic requirements for human survival, scarcity of water is thus an economic issue—does a particular use justify the costs of satisfying that use? "The definition of scarcity in noneconomic terms is a distraction that can lead to major misallocations of the water resource" (Rogers 1992). If social, political, or environmental objectives are set that cannot properly be quantified in economic terms, then these also are best evaluated in terms of their impact on economic welfare. No other satisfactory framework exists.

Market Failure in Water. Water has well known characteristics that lead to market failure. Investments are typically large and incur returns to box 1. The need for comprehensive approaches to water resource planning arises out of these concepts, notably water's unitary and variable nature together with market failure in water, which requires government intervention in the management of the resource. It is important to understand what "comprehensive" means in this context. It does not mean that governments must control each and every aspect of resource management. Many important activities are preferably decentralized to autonomous local, private, and user group entities. Indeed as a general principle, functions that can be done better at a lower level should not be done at a higher level.

Nor does it mean that governments alone should set objectives and priorities. Evidence worldwide suggests that participatory approaches involving stakeholders in decisionmaking result in more efficient and resilient solutions than those implemented by governments in isolation

---

scale—water supply is therefore a natural monopoly, and physical ('plumbing') constraints often limit transfers between uses. Moreover, renewable water is a fugitive and variable resource associated with pervasive externalities. It is thus inherently difficult to manage, becomes embedded in complex institutional structures, and cannot be apportioned and regulated solely—or even significantly—by the market. Thus, government is inevitably required to: (1) establish the policy, legislative, and regulatory framework for managing water supply and demand; and (2) ensure that water services are provided, notably by constructing large projects—dams, large scale irrigation, flood control—for which economies of scale or social externalities preclude private supply. The more effectively the framework evolves in response to changing conditions, and the more efficiently water services are provided, the lower will be the real costs of achieving national objectives.

The Economic Value of Water. Market failure precludes a clearing price for water that equates the real costs of its extraction with its value in the marginal use. "Shadow" estimates can be calculated for planning purposes so as to guide investment, pricing, and regulation policy. But shadow estimates are difficult to quantify and decisions are often taken with an inadequate understanding of real costs and values. Allocations frequently become locked into low-return uses (e.g., irrigation) and costly new projects are constructed. Even if countries are willing to incur subsidies to meet social, political, or environmental objectives, the full nature of such subsidies is seldom transparent and substantial costs are incurred inadvertently as a result of poor planning and decisionmaking.

from public opinion. Even so, market failure requires that government be ultimately responsible for resource management on behalf of its people, and water's unitary nature requires that such intervention take into account interactions in a comprehensive manner. In other words, interventions based on full consultation with stakeholders must still reflect sound planning. Even if markets can perform some allocation functions, this can only occur within a coherent and effective legislative and regulatory framework that, again, must be based on coherent—and comprehensive—planning.

Any rational choice between alternatives must reflect judgments that value alternative outcomes based on some common numeraire. Some outcomes may be difficult—even impossible—to quantify. But only if a specific objective overrides all others—preservation of a river in its natural state, the survival of a species—can some form of weighting be avoided either explicitly, using conventional multiobjective planning, or implicitly, as a consequence of the political process. If no attempt is made to attach values to such weights, then the powerful will deliberately or inadvertently distort the decisionmaking process in their own interests, resulting in inequities and hidden—and often substantial—subsidies and transfers. Even if political, social, and/or environmental objectives are difficult to measure, and even if cultural traditions or democratic pressures constrain government action, subsidies must still normally be constrained to socially acceptable levels. For this to be done in a rational manner, decisions must reflect a coherent valuation system and sound planning.

Experience with Water Resources Planning

Despite its importance, experience with water resources planning in the region has been mixed. In some countries, the focus has initially been on basin planning to verify the compatibility of programs and projects within the hydrological system. Basin plans have been or are being consolidated into national plans (e.g., in Iran and Morocco). In Egypt, the Nile basin comprises essentially the whole resource and has been subject to a variety of planning exercises. In Jordan, old national and regional plans are being updated with UNDP assistance. Major deficiencies in the region typically reside in long-term resource planning at the regional and basin levels, and their aggregation into national resource plans and long-term strategies. Reasons vary but can include ambiguous goals and objectives; inadequate data (box 2); insufficient staffing and financial resources; poorly executed studies; and, above all, a lack of political commitment to the results. Few countries in the region have

Box 2. Water Resources Data

Water resources data, in particular hydrological and hydrogeological data, are essential for planning, designing, and operating water projects. In most countries, specialized government services are responsible for the collection (measurement), transmission, processing (calculation of mean values, minima and maxima, frequencies of floods and droughts etc.), and publication of data.

Adequate planning and project preparation requires increasingly detailed data to evaluate all aspects that may affect a project and all possible effects of a project. Unfortunately, such data are often inadequate or unavailable because the capacity of hydrological agencies is, in many developing countries, hampered by a lack of funds, outdated equipment, low salaries and insufficiently trained staff. As a result, data are poorly recorded, data transmission from measuring stations to agency centers is unreliable, data processing and screening for inconsistencies and errors is inadequate, and the publication of data is often far behind schedule.

Modernization of hydrological work can help to reverse this decline: automatic measuring devices can provide more reliable and continuous recording of data, transmission by radio or satellite allows the immediate access to data and a remote control of the operation of the stations, and the use of computers together with specialized software facilitates data processing including the quality control of data. The use of automatic stations may also allow a reduction in the number of measuring stations. Satellite information/images of cloud cover, temperature, humidity, vegetation's response to rainfall etc. may then be used to fill "gaps" between stations.

In addition to hydrological and hydrogeological data, other water data are needed to prepare and operate water projects, such as data on operational performance of water systems, on its physical condition, on the cost of construction, operation, and maintenance, and on water charges and their collection. The collection and processing of such data can also be improved substantially by modern survey methods and equipment.

---

established effective mechanisms for public participation and consultation, and this again undermines commitment and implementation.

Israel and Tunisia are perhaps exceptions to this general disappointing picture in that both have created distribution systems that integrate water management over a substantial part of the national territory. The Water Security Project in Egypt aims to bring past planning efforts together in a coherent fashion, and similar attempts are being made in several other countries. Irrespective of past success or failure, however, the issue of effective planning cannot be avoided. The nature of the resource requires an analytical basis for sound decisionmaking. In turn, this requires a strong planning capability if the resource is to be successfully exploited and managed under conditions of growing scarcity and increasing pressures on its quality.

The Planning Horizon

The years 2000 and 2010 may seem to be in the distant future. However, the intervening period is relatively short given that it typically takes from five to ten years or more to plan, design, finance, build, and start up major water development projects. Conservation programs and efforts to induce changes in water use behavior similarly can have very long gestation periods. Moreover, as the limits of renewable resources are approached, the uncertainty associated with resource estimates become increasingly significant. Inadequate monitoring, information, and planning systems can result in unexpected and costly deficits and disruptions. A long-term horizon—twenty-five to fifty years—is thus unavoidable in water resource planning. Only if this is recognized can the costs of such deficits and disruptions be anticipated and controlled.

Supply Management

Water development projects include the construction of dams, reservoirs, wells, pumps, canals, and so forth. Surface supplies are typically exploited first. As accessibility to new surface sources decreases, and projects become more expensive (box 3), other sources including ground water become of greater significance. Ultimately, as renewable freshwater approaches full exploitation, nonconventional sources, such as wastewater treatment, water imports and, desalination, may become the only sources of new supply.

Surface storage adds to freshwater supply to the extent that it controls flooding and captures water otherwise lost to the sea and other sinks but, as rivers approach full exploitation, the additional yield from providing storage may be more than offset by evaporation losses from reservoir surfaces. Indeed, reservoirs built on the Nile, Euphrates, and Tigris substantially reduce renewable supplies in the region, for example, 14 percent of the Nile flow is lost to evaporation at Aswan. Even so, although the potential for further dam construction in MENA is limited, where justified, the control they provide over the timing and location of water can be critical to converting uncertain water endowments into reliable supplies.

Box 3. *Unit Costs of New Development*

The costs of new supplies are rising rapidly in the region. Jordan is an illustrative example. Estimates quoted in recent reports include the following:

Average incremental cost (AIC)

Agricultural users in the Jordan valley	US $0.23 per cubic meters
Wastewater treatment to Amman	US $0.37 per cubic meters
Groundwater exploitation in Amman	US $0.41 per cubic meters
Pumping surface water from the Jordan Valley	US $1.00 per cubic meters
Supply to Amman from the proposed Unity Dam	US $1.20 per cubic meters

While these estimates are not strictly comparable, they provide a useful indication of the range of costs encountered and how they are increasing. The costs of supply from the proposed Unity Dam are comparable to those of seawater desalination, which are about US $1.0–1.5 per cubic meters excluding the costs of water transport (although indications are that costs of desalination may be declining even below these levels). Other examples include groundwater costs in Israel, which range from US $0.03 per cubic meters for low-lift, small-distance schemes to US$0.50 per cubic meters for high-lift, long-distance schemes; wastewater treatment costs, which are quoted at between US$0.12 per cubic meters in Morocco and Tunisia to US$0.40 per cubic meters in the Gulf States; and the expected long-run marginal cost of raw water supplies in Algeria of US$0.39 per cubic meters, giving an average incremental cost (AIC) in urban uses of US$0.70 per cubic meters including distribution costs and US$0.49 per cubic meters in irrigation.

These costs can be compared with the value of water in agricultural production. Assuming one kilogram of wheat requires 1 cubic meter of water, then a very approximate estimate of value-added per unit of water in wheat production might be in the order of $0.05–0.10 per cubic meter, depending on the contribution of rainfall. In other words, the ratio of the value of wheat to the cost of desalination is very roughly in the order of 1:25 to 1:50. Value-added in more intensive crops quoted in recent reports ranges from US$0.12 to 0.35 per cubic meter (Morocco—gravity irrigation); from US$0.10 to 0.29 per cubic meter (Israel—gravity irrigation); and from US$0.53 to 0.89 per cubic meter (Israel—drip irrigation). While high-return irrigated agriculture can justify substantially more expensive water supply projects than traditional agriculture, the high costs of modern onfarm infrastructure must be added to those of rising costs of raw water. In many cases, therefore, agricultural activities will be unable to justify projected long-run marginal costs.

Relative to many other parts of the world, MENA is already critically dependent on groundwater, at least outside the major river valleys of the Nile and the Tigris/Euphrates. In some countries, it is already the predominant source of supply. It comprises essentially the only naturally occurring freshwater resource in Saudi Arabia and the Gulf States, and accounts for about 50 percent of freshwater abstractions in Jordan and 55 percent in Israel. Though recharge rates and flows are not always well known, the quantity and quality of groundwater is of increasing concern. Overpumping has led to rapid declines in watertables in many locations. Saline intrusion and pollution from urban and industrial wastewater are commonly encountered and reversible only at great cost.

Box 4. Nonconventional Sources of Water

Treated wastewater. The potential for the use of treated wastewater in irrigation has been reviewed in detail in a recent report (World Bank 1993). This report concluded that wastewater reuse can both add to water supply and have important environmental benefits provided use is carefully controlled. Total wastewater flows are rising rapidly, and although in most countries they will remain small relative to total renewable resources, in the water short countries of the Arabian peninsula they may represent the predominant long-term water supply for intensive irrigated agriculture. Substantial areas are already developed in several countries (Israel, Jordan, and Saudi Arabia) and pilot projects are spread widely throughout the region. In some countries (Morocco, Egypt) untreated wastewater is used despite its health impacts. The costs of wastewater treatment are quoted in the report at between US$0.12 and 0.40 per cubic meter depending on the technologies employed, which compares favorably not only with desalination (see below) but also with the more expensive interbasin transfer schemes. While health standards must be met if water is to be used directly in irrigation, the additional costs in some circumstances may be little more than required to meet normal environmental standards.

Desalination. Desalination is already an important source of supply in Saudi Arabia, the Gulf States, and Malta. Saudi Arabia alone accounts for 30 percent of world capacity with the rest of the Middle East accounting for a comparable amount. In Malta, desalination accounts for perhaps 50 percent of total water supply. Desalination remains expensive although recent cost reductions combined with the rising cost of conventional sources are making it surprisingly competitive in some situations. Since costs increase with the salinity of the water used, brackish waters—widely dispersed in MENA—provide a less costly alternative than seawater. Many factors, including the cost of capital

Groundwater abstractions approach or exceed renewable limits in many countries including Yemen, Israel, Jordan, Saudi Arabia, and the Gulf States. In others, pressures at the regional level may be equally acute, notably in the Maghreb. Potential for further abstractions still exists, for instance, in some parts of Iran, Iraq, and Egypt. But in the latter two countries recharge is almost wholly from major rivers and, though a shift from surface supplies to groundwater may reduce evaporation losses from waterlogged areas, it does not otherwise add to supply.

Nonconventional water sources include wastewater treatment and reuse, desalination, and water imports (box 4). They are typically (much) more expensive than conventional sources although, in the case of

---

and energy and the quality of the raw water, influence the choice of technology. Distillation is usually preferred for seawater (costs are currently about US$1.0–1.5 per cubic meter), and reverse osmosis and electrodialysis for brackish waters (US$0.4–0.8 per cubic meter). Large-scale desalination is invariably associated with low-cost energy and use of solar energy may one day become competitive. Provided that energy is assured, desalinated water provides a very much more predictable and reliable source than renewable supplies and avoids many of the management problems associated with the latter.

Water Imports. Various alternatives have been suggested for importing water into the region. They include the alternative "peace" pipeline projects for delivering water from surplus river basins in Turkey to various locations in the region; importation of water by tug or tanker or—more exotically—in icebergs towed from arctic regions; and the construction of the Jonglei canal in southern Sudan to increase the flow of the White Nile through reducing evaporation losses in the Sudd marshes. Each of these alternatives carries with it high costs. Moreover, in the case of the pipeline and tanker alternatives, the recipient country is dependent on others and many countries may be unwilling to expose themselves to the risks that this implies, given the difficult political problems facing the region. Nevertheless, as conventional sources are exploited, they may become economic in the longer term. Broad preliminary estimates of the costs of the peace pipeline suggest that they might be in the order of US$0.8–1.0 per cubic meter, which could make deliveries competitive with desalinated supplies even though financing problems will be formidable, and construction could take a decade. A feasibility study of the import of water from Turkey to Israel by sea estimated costs at US$0.22 per cubic meter although the proposed method—tugs dragging water in bags—has still to be proven technically feasible. The alternative of conventional tankers is estimated at more than US$1.00 per cubic meter.

30   A STRATEGY FOR MANAGING WATER IN THE MENA REGION

wastewater treatment, costs may largely be offset against environmental objectives and the need to safeguard other sources of supply. Political objections to large water transfer projects from outside the region and/or across national boundaries may prove insurmountable, and their financing and implementation would in any case pose formidable problems. Moreover, given the potential for reallocation from irrigation to other uses, the real costs of massive basin transfer projects or of large scale desalination will in most cases be economically hard to justify.

Real-Time Management of Supplies

Improved management of existing supplies can often be a partial alternative to investment in new supply. Plans of operation and maintenance (POMs) are an essential prerequisite for planning at both basin and project levels. For a variety of reasons, however, planning for operation and maintenance is often deficient, and standards of service often fall short of expected levels. In such cases, subsequent improvements in real-time management—for instance through improved joint operation of basinwide facilities, conjunctive use of surface and groundwater, or strengthened O&M at the project level—can often provide a very cost-effective means of increasing freshwater supplies. In some cases, however, improvements in real-time management are dependent on the integration of different water systems, which may be prohibitively costly.

Reallocation of Supplies

Reallocation between uses is a key—perhaps the key—mechanism for adjusting to water constraints. Irrigation accounts for perhaps 80 percent of water use, so relatively small transfers from agriculture would substantially increase availability to other sectors. For example, a 5 percent transfer from irrigation in Morocco could almost double total supplies available to the domestic sector. In Jordan, domestic uses already account for about 30 percent of total withdrawals but, even so, a 5 percent transfer from agriculture would still be equivalent to perhaps 15 percent of current domestic use.

However, few countries have been willing to commit themselves to a policy for the planned reallocation of water from irrigation to domestic and industrial use, even where governments recognize in principle the long-term inevitability of such a trend. Reasons vary but are often compelling. Withdrawal of water from irrigation in arid areas destroys the viability of agriculture. Not only may the multiplier effects and costs to third parties be very substantial but governments are also very reluctant to accept depopulation of rural areas and migration to urban areas already often under extreme stress. Moreover, most MENA countries are already deficient in basic food production and further dependence on imports carries risks that are politically very difficult to accept. Thus, many governments continue to project increases in irrigated areas, despite also recognizing the severity of water constraints, arguing that this is essential for food security and regional development. Unable to keep pace with the demands of expanding urban conglomerations, governments see irrigation as the means of retaining significant populations in otherwise unproductive regions.

There is much substance to these arguments. A priori it is often impossible to know whether the externalities associated with retaining water in irrigation will be positive or negative. Where irrigated agriculture provides the basis for regional economic activity, a full equilibrium analysis of the regional economy and its relationship to the national economy may in principle be required to be certain whether reallocation is economically justified although, in practice, such an exercise is seldom practicable. In some cases the spread of urban areas on to irrigated land will itself release irrigated water for other uses. Since urban consumption per hectar is typically less than evapotranspiration by crops, the effect on water availability is on balance positive. In Egypt, for instance—subject to issues of water quality—the water balance within the Nile basin could in theory take care of itself. It is the development of new land and transfers out of the Nile basin (e.g., to Sinai) that threatens water shortages early in the next century. But in most MENA countries, reallocation of water from agriculture will be inevitable. In the absence of effective market mechanisms, governments will have to be responsible, and the costs of reallocation will be primarily determined by whether governments do this in a coherent or an ad hoc manner.

Demand Management

Demand management can take many forms, from direct measures to control water use, to indirect measures that affect voluntary behavior (market mechanisms, financial incentives, public awareness programs). Price distortions in particular often magnify both scarcity and water quality problems. Low water charges encourage consumption and waste. Low water charges also put pressure on O&M budgets, leading to poor water treatment and further deterioration in water quality. Trade, macro, and input pricing distortions also can pose a threat to water supplies and water quality, for instance by failing to discourage industrial pollution (hazardous waste and wastewater discharges). Inefficiently low fertilizer prices similarly lead to increased fertilizer consumption and degradation of water supplies.

As in the case of planning, failure to implement demand management measures in the past does not negate their essential justification. The mix of possible measures will of course vary according to circumstance but in all cases the aim should be to increase the efficiency—and perhaps equity—of water use. Efficiency is, however, a relative concept and must reflect all the interactions in the water cycle (Bhatia and others 1993). For instance, irrigation efficiencies at the farm or scheme level may be relatively low, but, if losses recharge groundwater or are reused via the drainage system, basin efficiency can be much higher. Scheme-level efficiencies in Egypt are, for instance, notoriously low by the standards of other countries in the region, but annual average efficiency in the Nile basin from Aswan to the sea is estimated at 65 percent—comparable to the efficiency of modern pipe systems at the project level—and this reaches 80 percent in summer when water demands reach their peak. The potential for water savings in irrigation—although considerable—may thus in some cases be lower than is commonly supposed. Modernization of irrigation schemes may still be justified in terms of improved standards of service; reductions in pumping, treatment, or other costs; or water savings in schemes close to the sea. But only if evaporation is reduced or flows to unusable sinks decline—the sea, saline aquifers, polluted rivers—will true water savings be achieved.

Public Awareness

Transparency and accountability are best established within the context of participatory approaches designed to ensure that stakeholder views are reflected in decisionmaking and to secure public commitment and support. Appeals to the public through public awareness campaigns, education programs, and similar initiatives have also led to significant changes in human behavior related to water conservation and use, notably in developed countries. While their potential is less well established in developing countries, they clearly have an important role to play and, since they are in large measure costless, they should invariably receive priority and should always accompany other programs to increase efficiency and/or conserve supplies.

Water Efficiency Improvements

Reduction in water losses is important to any demand management program. Unaccounted-for-water can reach as high as 50 to 60 percent in urban delivery systems and, while some losses can be recycled, loss reduction is always a first priority. Leak detection and repair programs, identification of illegal connections, and reduction in system pressure can all play a part. Many low water-use devices and technologies are available—small supply pipes, restricted faucets and shower heads and so forth—although adoption of such devices in MENA countries has to date been limited. Efficiency in industrial uses in developed countries has been typically forced by water quality standards that have led many industries to recirculate their process water, resulting in substantial reductions in industrial water demand.

Technical interventions to reduce water use have particular potential in irrigation. Canal lining and improved conveyance technologies can save water in the order of 10 to 30 percent (whether similar savings are achieved at the basin level is a matter for specific study). At the farm level, surface irrigation can be improved through land levelling and the introduction of better onfarm practices or can be replaced by sprinkler or micro irrigation (e.g., drip) techniques. Micro irrigation in particular has potential for major savings. These can be in the order of 30 to 50 percent compared to surface irrigation, even allowing for the necessary allocation for leaching of salts, since only a fraction of the soil is wetted and evaporation is thus directly reduced. However, drip irrigation is expensive to the farmer and dependent on a very reliable source of supply. If successfully introduced, productivity typically also rises markedly, in particular if it is combined with delivery of fertilizer and other chemicals. Yield increases have proven to be the decisive incentive for the spread of drip systems where conditions are appropriate. For instance, drip now accounts for more than 90 percent of all irrigation in Israel and has resulted in sharp reductions in agricultural water use. Comparable trends are occurring in Jordan. Pilot projects are widely spread throughout the region and both government and private sector initiatives are beginning to have considerable impact.

Regulatory Measures

The most direct regulation is to mandate water use. Quantitative restrictions are, however, difficult to administer although specific prohibitions (e.g., on garden watering, or car washing) may be easier to police. Rationing or rotational deliveries can achieve a comparable effect and are commonly adopted during droughts or where demand exceeds the physical capacity of the system. In surface irrigation schemes, rotational delivery can become more permanent and, provided farmers know in advance the expected pattern of delivery, creates a strong incentive to maximize the returns to (scarce) supplies. Direct controls on cropping are an alternative which in principle could reduce water consumption at the farm level. However, mandated cropping patterns constrain a farmer's ability to respond to market signals and may thus have perverse effects on agricultural value added.

The regulation of groundwater exploitation is a universal but often intractable problem. Most countries issue extraction permits although—with the partial exceptions of Israel and neighboring Cyprus—these have seldom been able to prevent uncontrolled overdrafts, since only a few countries in the region have the administrative capacity for direct controls. Groundwater regulation can also be approached indirectly (e.g., by regulating the spacing of wells or the number of drilling rigs). However, there are few examples in the region—or the world—where such approaches have proved entirely satisfactory. Financial constraints related to the costs of pumping and well yield are thus normally the ultimate control. Provided that inputs (equipment, power, energy, and credit) and outputs (crops, industrial products) are priced at their true cost, and there are no adverse externalities such as saline intrusion, this may indeed result in an economically efficient solution. In some cases, this will lead to the mining of the resource. While this may be economically justified, it is inherently temporary and, if the activity is to continue, replacement resources will ultimately have to be found.

Regulation of water quality standards has been widely adopted, indeed many governments have adopted overambitious targets that they have found difficult to enforce. Point sources of pollution are relatively easy to monitor by an environment ministry or agency although, if standards are set too high, the costs of meeting them can create strong incentives for noncompliance. Nonpoint pollution, notably from fertilizers and pesticides, has proven a much more intractable problem worldwide. Specific pesticides can be banned, and prices can be established at levels which discourage excessive use, but few mechanisms are available that account in full for all externalities.

Financial Incentives

Financial interventions should typically be governed by two important principles gaining support worldwide: the user-pays principle and the polluter-pays principle. In most cases, not only are these seen to be equitable—and therefore gain public acceptance—but they also tend to result in economically efficient solutions. Few MENA countries have, however, made systematic use of such mechanisms and, where they have attempted to do so, administrative weaknesses have often resulted in failure in implementation. Israel is an exception that has adopted rigid demand-side measures dating at least from the early 1970s, in part in the context of Bank-supported projects. Cyprus is another exception from outside the MENA region.

Water charges have typically been looked at as a mechanism for financing the O&M costs of the water agency rather than as a demand management measure to encourage efficiency in water use or reallocate water from low-return to high-return uses. So long as extraction costs remain reasonably constant and externalities are limited, pricing to meet full cost recovery approximates to marginal cost pricing. But as costs rise and external impacts mount, the efficiency or opportunity cost price typically rises well above the level needed to meet cost recovery objectives. Market failure limits the role of price in allocation and precludes the emergence of a clearing price that equates the real costs of its extraction with its value in the marginal use (box 1). Pricing that allows for externalities would, nevertheless, still provide the correct incentives for efficient use, and the Bank has long encouraged governments to bring resource pricing progressively closer to real economic levels on the user-pays and polluter-pays principles.

In practice, water charges are normally well below levels needed to recover financial costs let alone for rising marginal costs and externalities, being set at levels that do not signal the real importance or value of water. In Algeria the long run marginal cost of water to urban consumers, including both raw water supply and distribution, is about US$0.52 per cubic meter compared to the average water charge of US$0.12 per cubic meter. The contrast is even more striking in irrigation: current water charges average US$0.02 per cubic meter compared to an average marginal water cost of US$0.32 per cubic meter. In Egypt the combined marginal cost of raw water supply and distribution ranges from US$0.03 per cubic meter for rural areas to US$0.25 in major urban centers though water charges for domestic consumers average no more than US$0.03 per cubic meter. To these costs must be added the cost of treating the wastewater collected by the sewer system: these costs range from an estimated US$0.12 per cubic meter in Morocco to US$0.37 per cubic meter in Jordan (for water reuse) and US$0.40 per cubic meter in the Gulf States. The public is therefore not aware of the economic value of water, has no incentive to conserve, and therefore cannot be expected to take responsibility for its protection or conservation.

Political objections and constraints to increasing water charges are often seen as insurmountable. But it is also true that the problems associated with achieving cost recovery objectives are frequently institutional in nature. Only if governments are willing to allow full financial

36 A STRATEGY FOR MANAGING WATER IN THE MENA REGION

autonomy and hold agencies accountable for performance, can significant improvements be anticipated (chapter 4). Although to date privatization of water supply utilities has made little headway in the region, private management—if not ownership—would probably provide the most effective way of achieving such objectives.

- *Urban utility pricing.* Most governments have the ostensible objective of setting water charges that will cover the O&M costs of urban utilities and in many cases also a proportion of capital costs. But in practice, they are often unwilling to implement their own policies so that revenues frequently fall short of those needed to cover O&M. Even in Jordan, where rates to the municipal consumer appear to approach the long run marginal cost of new supplies, unaccounted-for losses and other deficiencies require government subsidies to the water supply agencies. Elsewhere, even if in principle water use is measured and fees are charged according to the volume of water used, rates invariably fall below those required to have a significant impact on demand and administrative constraints limit the effectiveness of collection programs. Water supply services are usually publicly owned and there often exists a view that a certain level of water service should be provided at nominal cost to ensure that public health standards are maintained. While this view has some merit, supplies above basic requirements should still be charged at the true cost.
- *Irrigation water charges.* Water charges in irrigation are typically well below even the inadequate levels of the municipal sector and, in contrast to the municipal sector, many governments are unwilling to accept even the principle of irrigation cost recovery. Irrigation and other subsidies are often rationalized as a means of offsetting low farm prices controlled to keep down food prices in the cities. This argument has some merit and, certainly, any adjustment to input prices must reflect an understanding of all government pricing interventions and their impact on farm incomes. But free irrigation water sends the wrong signals to farmers and increased charges for irrigation water should almost invariably be an important element of general programs designed to get the prices right.

  Few countries have recognized the need to charge adequately for irrigation supplies. In Morocco the water law requires that all water consumption be subject to the payment of fees on a common basis even if, in practice, rates in irrigation continue to be well below those in urban areas. As in most countries, therefore, irrigation continues to be subsidized. In Jordan, little attempt is made to cover even O&M costs and irrigation water charges in the Jordan valley are a fraction of those charged to the municipal consumer. In Egypt and Yemen, where the irrigation agency is a line department, surface water supplies are provided free with the agency financed from taxes and other public revenues (although Yemen is committed under a Bank covenant to introduce irrigation service fees). Only in communal and private irrigation—e.g., in Yemen and Morocco—must costs be covered by members of the community or by a private entrepreneur and, even in these cases, government investment support can result in substantial capital subsidies.

Any meaningful increase in water charges would encourage economies in water use, for instance by encouraging farmers to invest in water-saving devices and technologies or to shift cropping patterns out of high water-using crops. Even satisfying cost recovery criteria would go some way to attaining demand management objectives. Moreover, the structure of charges can be designed to encourage water savings, besides reflecting differences in the level of service and/or equity objectives. Possibilities include decreasing or increasing block tariffs, seasonal or spatial differences, and contingent charges triggered by an external event such as a drought. Increasing block tariffs can provide for basic needs for the population at large and can be made compatible with opportunity cost principles at the margin, thus providing an important mechanism for reducing demand while satisfying social objectives.

Other financial incentives can also encourage appropriate action by private interests and consumers. Subsidies or tax rebates can encourage investment in water quality treatment—financed either through the general budget or from levies on water users—and penalties can be imposed on those that do not meet quality standards or quantity restrictions. Irrigation water use can be addressed in various ways, for instance through subsidies on micro irrigation equipment or by establishing crop water use standards—as in Israel—with penalties levied if standards are exceeded and financial rewards given if there are savings. Water use in Israel has been gradually squeezed in this way over time but, though such programs can prove very effective, they require administrative controls that are widely lacking elsewhere in the region.

Water Markets

Local water markets almost invariably emerge where private interests or individuals control particular water supplies or assets, and can deal directly with their customers. Examples include the sale of irrigation or domestic water from individually owned tubewells or pumps; the provision of domestic water by private tanker in urban areas poorly served by public supply; and exchange or sale of irrigation turns between farmers along a common channel. Such markets undoubtedly serve an important purpose in helping redistribute supplies—both from day to day and over longer periods—in accordance with the conditions of supply and demand. They should be facilitated to the extent possible wherever they serve an expressed need. The reallocation of supplies through market mechanisms in greater amounts, or over greater distances, or between major sectors, raises entirely different issues (see note 3). Tradable water rights at this level would require a system of property rights in water and contractual arrangements that is quite different from that prevalent in the MENA region, and it is difficult to envisage the emergence of such a system, at least in the foreseeable future.

Conclusions

The desirable balance between supply and demand management measures varies over time as conditions evolve. So long as conventional water sources are available, these can be exploited to meet most sectoral requirements. As water supplies are more fully utilized, greater emphasis is typically placed on demand management to postpone the need for increasingly costly new investment. Measures to increase efficiency and strengthen O&M are invariably a priority but the rapidity with which shortages are emerging in the MENA region means that many countries—Algeria, Jordan, Morocco, Yemen—will inevitably have to face the difficult issues associated with reallocation between uses. Desalination and other nonconventional sources can be an alternative to reallocation in countries able to afford the implied subsidies, but the costs of such a strategy are normally beyond the means of poorer countries except in limited contexts (e.g., in tourist areas, for satisfying cooling water demands by thermal electric power plants located on the sea coast, or in exceptional circumstances for urban areas located close to the coast).

This chapter has explored water resources policy alternatives facing governments in MENA countries. Difficult choices have to be made. As discussed further in chapter 5, the systematic preparation of national and international water strategies in association with local interests and stakeholders could help generate consensus on the choice of appropriate action programs. Preparation of such strategies is, however, no substitute for a permanent planning capacity that can provide the continuing analytical basis for guidance in the water sector. Nor will agreement on a strategy be sufficient in itself to ensure its successful implementation.

Weak institutions lie at the heart of most water resource management problems and, therefore, institutions in their widest sense must evolve to complement policy formulation and ensure its effective implementation. These issues are discussed in the following chapter.

Notes

1. There is no hard-and-fast distinction between supply and demand management. One definition classifies actions that affect the quantity and quality of water at the entry point in the distribution system as "supply management," and actions that influence the use or wastage of water after this point as "demand management": "this...roughly separates management actions into those which are orientated towards construction, engineering and operations (supply management), and those which tend to draw on social and behavior sciences (demand management)...there are exceptions in each case" (United Nations Department of Technical Cooperation 1991).

2. Government policy and public water distribution have been the predominant basis for water allocation even in countries where property rights in water are unambiguous, where contractual arrangements between water wholesalers and water retailers can be managed effectively in response to variable supplies, and where the legal and regulatory system can deal satisfactorily with third party and other effects. The reasons reflect the well-known characteristics of water, in particular those associated with market failure (box 1). In a few places (e.g., Australia, the western United States) market mechanisms complement public allocation policy and will almost certainly play an increasingly important role in future. However, it is misleading to assume that similar mechanisms will be possible in the foreseeable future in countries—such as those in the MENA region—where legal, institutional, and financial arrangements are weak; measurement and control of highly variable supplies is problematic; environmental regulation is ill developed; water charges are far below the economic value of water; and water is subject to the innumerable cultural, social, and political pressures associated with poor and rapidly growing populations living in sprawling urban areas and on tiny farms.

3. A new upstream project may deprive traditional downstream users. Modification of a reservoir's operating rules may give an increasing share of available supplies to one use (e.g., a water utility) at the expense of another (e.g., an irrigation scheme).

4. Institutional Issues

"Institutions" in the broadest sense comprise organizations (public/private), laws, regulations, decrees, customs, markets, and all that is associated with these. They largely determine whether objectives can in practice be achieved and the transition from a predominantly supply-side production strategy to a balanced strategy for managing both water supply and demand must therefore be matched by complementary institutional reform. Moreover the various institutional elements are interdependent and many deficiencies arise from inconsistencies between them. Though institutional change is usually incremental, it should occur within the context of devising effective arrangements for the entire water resources area.

The problems created by inefficient institutions are aggravated by the speed with which water scarcity and water quality problems have emerged. Arrangements put in place during periods of relative surplus by single-purpose users become increasingly inappropriate as scarcity and environmental pressures mount. Strong vested interests are fostered among those deriving benefit from the status quo and they can become formidable impediments to change. Moreover, water is often subject to religious and cultural sanctions. It may be allocated according to customs that are deeply ingrained and difficult to modify even if modern society creates unforeseen demands, and even if technical advance—e.g. mechanical pumps—leads to damaging pressures on the resource. The use of economic instruments that go beyond the recovery of the immediate costs of extraction is often a particular difficulty that meets strong resistance.

Institutional reform must be responsive to traditional norms and practices and, to the extent possible, should integrate these within new institutional structures. However, pressures of population and economic development have created unprecedented problems, and new regulatory and incentive practices are almost invariably required. Continued adoption of fragmented approaches would incur unacceptable costs. Coordinated approaches are thus universally essential even if details of reform programs must respond to the stage of development reached and the characteristics of the country concerned.

Legislation and Regulation

Legislation provides the basis for government regulation and operations, and establishes the context for action by nongovernment entities and individuals. Regulatory functions comprise monitoring and enforcement of established laws, agreements, rules, and standards.

Legislation

In many countries, legislation has tended to evolve ad hoc although those influenced by the French legal tradition often adopt comprehensive water codes (*codes de l'eau*). With growing scarcity, ad hoc approaches become increasingly unsatisfactory, and coherent management of the resource needs to be supported by coherent legislation. Indeed "recognition of water resource planning in legislation is perhaps the single most significant mechanism for sound decisionmaking in the management of water resources in the long run" (Burchi 1989).

Under Islamic law, water is a gift from God. In principle, it thus belongs to the community, creating a primary right for human and livestock use. However, value-added as a result of investments in distribution or conservation may create a qualified right to ownership and thus permit appropriation and local water marketing.

Sharing at times of scarcity varies according to local usage but the general approach is acknowledgement of the right of prior appropriation combined with local customs governing the distribution of any surplus. The essential traits of classical law were codified in the Ottoman civil code and, in countries influenced by France (e.g., Lebanon and the Maghreb), contributed to an holistic and comprehensive approach to water sharing. In countries influenced by Britain (e.g., the Gulf States, Egypt, Jordan, Yemen), legislation has tended to be more piecemeal and, with growing water scarcity, less satisfactory.

State property of water is an original right subject to varying recognition of community appropriation. Rights of companies and/or private individuals are therefore residual. State permits are generally required for private exploitation and the state is also responsible—either directly or through concession—for treatment, distribution, and major public works. Allocations and priorities are, however, often vaguely stated or are absent, and many uses—for instance, instream and other environmental uses—have mostly been overlooked. Moreover, few statutes set out the procedures to be followed in reallocating water to higher priority and/or higher value purposes, and thus reallocation tends to be unplanned in response to the pressure of events. A clear indication of government priorities in this respect is essential if the high cost associated with such ad hoc allocations is to be avoided. Such policies should also *inter alia* provide acceptable rules for handling year-to-year variability in precipitation and surface water flows.

Regulation

Among subjects covered to varying degrees are the administration of land and water rights, real-time allocations and standards of service, water quality and environmental aspects, and the configuration and safety of facilities. Many other regulatory functions also affect water, as other areas of the economy, including those governing civil service administration, markets, finance and audit, employment, and private enterprise. Regulatory functions are often weakly and inconsistently developed and applied in MENA countries. These weaknesses may be a reflection of factors that go well beyond the water area so that, in the real world, water resources management may often have to accept—and respond to—second-best conditions. Even so, enforcement of rights and standards is critical to successful water resource management and—to the extent feasible—improvements in administrative efficiency should receive high priority.

Agency Functions and Organization

All countries have numerous public and private agencies, organizations, and individuals involved in aspects of water management. In general, however, governments have dominated both water development and the provision of water services even if private initiative has often been significant at the local level. Historically, most public water agencies were established to meet a specific need, generally focusing on a single use; thus a country may typically have ministries or departments dealing with irrigation, agriculture, fisheries and wildlife, transport, energy, environment, health and human resources, and so on, each involved with one aspect of water use. Specific activities related to that use—e.g., the provision of water services to end-users—may be delegated to autonomous entities reporting to the parent department. In such cases, the department and its subsidiary agencies together usually cover all aspects of the single use, including data collection and analysis, planning, construction of facilities, and operation, maintenance, and replacement.

INSTITUTIONAL ISSUES 43

Each single-purpose agency impinges on management of the common resource according to its own needs and biases. If water supply greatly exceeds demand, fragmented arrangements can be effective in carrying out specific assignments. However, such fragmentation is inefficient and inadequate in an environment of competing uses for scarce supplies. The issues involved are complex and country-specific but they can be usefully considered in relation to: (i) the management of the resource, and (ii) the provision of water services.

- *Management of the resource* typically involves policy development, supply planning, allocation, permit administration, and environmental management, and is predominantly a government function. However, this should not preclude private participation to ensure accountability and responsiveness to the interests of stakeholders in the resource. Nor does it imply that all functions should be concentrated at the center. Indeed, as a general principle, functions should not be exercised at a higher level if they can be better exercised at a lower level.
- *Delivery of water services* involves the wholesaling of water to intermediaries and the retail distribution of water to end-users—farmers in an irrigation scheme, households in a municipality, industries and hotels, and so on. Delivery of water services can be either a public or a private function and, as in the case of resource management, should—to the extent possible and subject to economies of scale considerations—be delegated to lower levels and local entities. Whether in the private or public sectors, delivery of service is usually best assigned to autonomous agencies (utilities) that deliver specific services for a fee.

Delivery of water services in MENA countries has predominantly been undertaken by public agencies. However, emphasis on private participation has grown worldwide, and increased private sector involvement is warranted especially in the operation of water and sewerage utilities. Private firms depend for their survival on their reputation for performance; they assume legal liability for the consequences of any professional negligence; and, by definition, they are financially autonomous. These factors provide powerful incentives for supplying cost-effective and high-quality services. Such incentives are weak or nonexistent in most public sector agencies, which usually feature nearly total employment security, promotion by seniority, and lack of accountability and appropriate sanctions in the case of poor performance. The direct consequences can include the construction of high-cost, low-quality facili-

44   A STRATEGY FOR MANAGING WATER IN THE MENA REGION

ties and the poor delivery of service. Indirect effects can include a weak professional labor force. Privatization in the water supply and sanitation subsector thus could have a major role in greatly improving efficiency.

In contrast to the urban sector, there are few opportunities for private commercial involvement in the provision of irrigation services, though there is a long history of schemes managed by farmers in the region (e.g., in Morocco and Yemen). The transfer of smaller public schemes to farmer management, and delegation of O&M responsibilities to water-user groups in larger schemes, both have considerable potential. Moreover in some countries (e.g., Morocco), it is possible to envisage the long-term transformation of autonomous public bodies into private entities managed by users along commercial lines in a manner comparable to the irrigation districts typical of many developed countries.

Management of the Resource

Water management can be considered at the national, regional, basin, and local levels. At each level, the logical management of water as a unitary resource (box 1) requires functional linkages in agency responsibilities for: (1) water and associated land use, (2) surface and subsurface water, and (3) water quantity and water quality. In practice, agency responsibilities are often fragmented and associated with the user or interest that had a predominant role at previous stages of development. Consolidation of responsibilities in an holistic resource management structure thus often conflicts with existing vested interests. Three general principles are highly desirable in assigning responsibilities for management of the unified resource:

- Separation of policy, planning, and regulatory functions from operational activities at each level of government
- Assignment of operations to specialist agencies where appropriate
- Decentralizationtion of functional responsibility to the appropriate level.

National Policy and Planning

Many countries have established centralized mechanisms for policy and planning. Typically, overall control and coordination are exercised by a council, comprising senior officials from different ministries and departments involved in aspects of water, supported by a professional secretariat. The council may be chaired at the highest level of government (for instance, in Morocco by the King), reflecting the political importance of water and the high priority attached to water issues by many MENA governments.

The creation of centralized policy and planning mechanisms is a logical and necessary step for comprehensive and coordinated management of unitary water resources. In practice, however, such centralized arrangements are frequently underfinanced, understaffed and, despite their apparent high position in government, may lack real operational authority. Councils meet infrequently and their secretariats may be weakened by opposition from line agencies who see them as operational intrusions. This lack of success should not, however, negate the essential justification of coordinated resource planning. Not only should national planning mechanisms be above sectoral agencies, for instance in the office of the prime minister or minister of finance or planning, but there must be commitment and authority to formulate policy and to ensure that water programs and projects are in practice consistent with national policies and plans.

Tunisia and Israel are examples of countries that have benefited from effective centralized institutional arrangements supported by water sector master planning. While there have still been biases—for instance in Israel the ministry of agriculture has been predominant in water matters—this has contributed to rational investment decisions, relatively efficient management of the resource, and effective assistance programs. In contrast, despite master planning activities (e.g., in Egypt), or the creation of high-level policy councils (e.g., in Yemen), in many other countries the will to make hard choices has been lacking and major avoidable costs have undoubtedly been incurred.

Regional and Basin Entities

Resource management is logically exercised at the river-basin level and several countries (e.g., Jordan, Yemen, and Morocco) have decentralized water resource management functions to regional or river-basin authorities. These arrangements have met with mixed success. In contrast to national policy and planning agencies, such entities are often relatively well financed and well staffed since they are often assigned the authority to plan and implement multipurpose projects and programs within their jurisdictions. As a result, they are often powerful organizations and encroach on—and may be in conflict with—national policies. Until recently, Jordan provided a good illustration. Although the Ministry of Irrigation and Water was intended to be responsible for policy and planning, in practice the Jordan Valley Authority and the Water Authority of Jordan divided national planning between them. Since these agencies are also responsible for delivering water to end-users (customers, farmers etc.), this confused resource management with water service functions. Jordan has recently taken the important step of separating water policy development from operations by strengthening the ministry's policy formulation capacity while leaving service implementation to the operational agencies. In general, policy and strategy should remain a central government function even if it is often essential to delegate planning and management functions to regional entities at the level of the basin or hydrological unit.

Regulation and Oversight

Monitoring and enforcement of water quantity allocations, water quality standards, and environmental regulations logically takes place at the level of resource ownership and management—e.g., at the basin or hydrological unit level. However, some powers can be properly delegated to lower levels of government, for instance those governing land use, administrative and financial supervision of service organizations, and groundwater. Environmental and water quality standards are often set by an environmental ministry or similar organization with powers to regulate the activities of a wide range of private and public entities. This arrangement can work well so long as the ministry confines its activities to regulation, with powers delegated to local offices as appropriate. But there is a tendency for such agencies to initiate special environmental investment programs in parallel with those of traditional line agencies. This negates the principle of the separation of regulation and operations and can lead to waste, duplication, and ambiguity in operations.

Data Responsibilities

There is merit in consolidating collection and analysis of hydrological data within a single agency to overcome the costs of duplication and the dangers of fragmentation associated with each water agency gathering its own information. The centralized data bank should of course be open to all public agencies and authorized agencies operating within the country. In order to assure the integrity of the data, it is desirable that the assigned agency should be devoid of project planning or operational responsibilities. Detailed hydrological data may still be collected by specialized agencies, for instance large irrigation or hydropower authorities. The many other types of data required in water resources planning and management must also be accessible to government and nongovernment agencies (box 2).

Delivery of Water Services

Delivery of water services includes wholesale conveyance and transfer of raw water as well as retail delivery to households, industries, farms, and other end-users. Different sectors have very different requirements. Nevertheless, comparable principles underlie the successful delivery of services in all sectors.

Water Services as Utilities

Experience worldwide has shown that measurable economic services—delivery of raw water supplies, domestic water supply and sewerage, irrigation, power, telecommunications—are best provided by autonomous entities organized as utilities delivering defined services to customers for a fee. The entity owns assets, procures new facilities and equipment, finances capital improvements and undertakes O&M. It can be a national agency, local government entity, user association or private company although—as previously argued—private sector structures often have the potential for greater efficiency than those in the public domain.

Whether private or public, the delivery of many water services is best decentralized to the local level. However, such local entities may be numerous and will normally require support. Typically therefore a national line agency or corporation should undertake strategic planning for the sector and provide policy guidance and technical support to individual utilities. Where the latter are public entities, budgeting and accounting should be clearly separated from the parent ministry or department. Where they are private entities, they would normally be regulated under standard financial and industrial safety procedures. By isolating the service function from other influences and activities, the utility form promotes operational efficiency, service accountability, and sound financial management. Taxes and subsidies can be clarified, and the basis for effective public scrutiny and operational transparency can be established. The alternative to a utility form is generally a line department—national, regional, or local—financed from taxes and other government revenues. Such an arrangement may be necessary if service to an individual user is difficult to measure—e.g., for flood protection, river training, and so on—but is undesirable where the service is readily quantified.

Water Wholesaling Agencies

Despite the theoretical advantages, few multipurpose facilities in MENA are operated by autonomous entities that wholesale water to different

48 A STRATEGY FOR MANAGING WATER IN THE MENA REGION

users. An exception, perhaps, is the national water carrier in Israel. More typically, such facilities are operated by a line department (as in the case of the Aswan High Dam in Egypt) or by a predominant user (e.g., a power, irrigation, or water supply agency) that allocates water to other users in line with government policy. If the predominant user is organized as a utility, it can still provide a wholesaling service to other users for a fee and, in principle, achieve most of the advantages of a specialized agency.

Urban Water Supply and Sewerage

Urban water supply in MENA is almost invariably provided by autonomous public entities. In practice, however, autonomy may be more apparent than real since such entities are often closely controlled by government, for instance in matters relating to fee setting, personnel, and investment policy. In some cases (e.g., in Jordan and Yemen) the parent ministry has essentially absorbed the organization back into a civil service structure. Where this occurs, incentives for efficient delivery of service can be weakened resulting in administrative, financial, and technical problems.

Reform programs normally emphasize the need to reestablish full autonomy, notably in respect of personnel management, tariffs, investment programming decisions, and financing. The Bank's experience in Morocco, however, where successive projects have failed to achieve their ostensible objectives, illustrates the difficulty that governments have in implementing such reform programs in the public sector. Privately managed utilities no doubt in principle can deliver services more efficiently and at lower cost. However, political objections, weak regulatory frameworks, and the poor financial condition of existing public agencies, typically rule out the full privatization of assets except in special cases such as tourism areas. Other options exist, however, such as concession arrangements, service or management contracts, or BOT (build, operate, and transfer) schemes. These would appear to have considerable potential in the region and should undoubtedly assume a greater role.

Sewerage and waste water treatment have been given far less attention worldwide than water supply. In urban areas, sewerage is normally a subsidiary responsibility of the water supply utility although it can also be provided independently by a public line department or utility. However, fee collection is often feasible only in association with water deliveries so that combining water supply and sanitation may be a condition for creating an autonomous utility. Sanitation programs must also be closely aligned with the regulation of water quality, while wastewater treatment programs need to be planned in close association with potential users (e.g., irrigators). As water scarcity intensifies, wastewater reuse becomes of greater significance. Indeed, in the most water-short countries, it will ultimately become the predominant source of irrigation supply, at least in the vicinity of urban areas. While the utility form in both the supply and use of treated wastewater will continue to have decisive advantages, difficult and interconnected issues of water quality, cost recovery, and health and environmental control, require that the entities involved operate within a strong regulatory context.

Rural Water Supply

Direct line department provision of rural water supply services predominates in many countries, reflecting the social objectives that typically characterize rural water supply programs. Cost recovery measures may be politically and practically difficult to institute and large scale government subsidies may be inevitable. Indeed, the costs of extending safe and secure water supply in rural areas is often a major development challenge. Creation of autonomous regional entities can help strengthen administration and clarify subsidy levels. Moreover, it is being increasingly recognized that the transfer of small-scale facilities to village and local user groups has many advantages related to effective O&M and minimizing the burden on the government exchequer.

Irrigation

In Egypt, Iraq, and Yemen, public irrigation has been traditionally provided free to the end-user by line departments (though Yemen is committed to the introduction of a user fee under a Bank covenant). In common with other parts of the world that have a line department structure in public irrigation, this adversely affects financial accountability and the use of user charges as an efficiency signal. Major—and politically difficult—reform of the irrigation agencies, including the handover of major responsibilities to financially autonomous entities and user groups, may therefore be a necessary precondition for achieving many efficiency and accountability objectives.

In other countries—e.g., Morocco, Jordan, Algeria—public irrigation is already the responsibility of autonomous organizations comparable to those in the municipal sector. In principle this provides incentives for efficient delivery of irrigation services, and to some extent this is the case in practice. However, their freedom of action is typically even more limited than for urban utilities. There are also major constraints on how

50 A STRATEGY FOR MANAGING WATER IN THE MENA REGION

far such entities can be privatized even if communal schemes (e.g., in Yemen and Morocco) are already managed by autonomous village organizations. In public irrigation schemes, water users associations (WUAs) are being promoted (e.g., in Tunisia and Morocco) and have been successfully introduced in many other parts of the world. Generally, their responsibilities have been limited to the O&M of tertiary systems. In some countries, water user associations are federated for O&M of larger canals and for participation in overall system management, and the potential for full transfer of smaller public schemes can often be considered. The enabling legislation for WUAs in some countries provides for other responsibilities (e.g., for drainage, tubewells, procurement of agricultural inputs, and marketing of products, as well as authority to borrow funds and finance applicable operations). In these cases they can approximate to traditional multipurpose cooperative types of organization.

Other Water Services

Local drainage, flood control, and river training facilities can be incorporated within the responsibilities of an irrigation scheme or an urban or regional utility. However, larger scale facilities are generally provided by national, regional, or local government departments with few effective means for cost recovery or financial autonomy. Recreational and environmental services are relatively ill developed in the MENA region. To the extent that they are provided, they are also largely the responsibility of the public sector other than in high-visibility tourist areas. Other economic services include river transport and similar services (often provided by public or private utilities or companies), and aquaculture and fisheries (usually a private activity). These are all predominantly instream uses which require flow regulation and maintenance of water quality standards. Charging for such services has proven problematic, and they are seldom a significant item in the budget of the respective entities.

Staff Capability and Training

Public water sector staff capability in MENA varies considerably from country to country. However, there are some generalizations that fit most cadres. Generally, water staff are trained as engineers and openings for those with other required disciplines are severely limited with few opportunities for promotion. The level of staff capability and motivation varies but low salaries and benefits generally undermine morale and discourage adoption of modern technologies and management systems. Poor compensation frequently fosters an environment in which staff look to other income from water users and contractors, with consequent adverse effects on efficiency. It is particularly difficult to get qualified staff posted to important planning, design and research positions. As a result, much of the planning is done by consultants and many countries do not have sufficient qualified interdisciplinary staff even to review and comment on the work of consultants. Indeed, governments may have surprisingly limited input into development plans that go forward for authorization.

Training and staff development should undoubtedly have high priority. However, they are unlikely to be fully effective if they are not associated with incentives that motivate staff to improve performance. While the utility concept in principle provides such a framework for rewarding performance and improving incentives and financial accountability, it is usually more difficult to create appropriate conditions in government agencies responsible for important resource planning and management activities. This is an important issue that cannot be avoided. If incentives are inadequate to attract high-calibre planning staff, MENA countries cannot be expected to overcome their complex water resource management problems.

International Issues

Many water issues in MENA are international in nature. Formal treaties in principle can provide a mechanism for establishing surface water rights and making productive coordinated development possible. However, out of the 286 international water treaties worldwide, only one major agreement is from the MENA region—that for the Nile. Moreover, even this agreement is limited to the two lower riparians and has relatively ill-developed organizational arrangements for implementing joint management and development programs (chapter 2). In the case of other systems—notably the Tigris/Euphrates, the Jordan, and the Orontes—partial understandings between one or more of the riparians have played some role but there are few legally binding treaties. There are no significant agreements for shared aquifers and development of these resources by one or more riparians can therefore take place without regard to any impact on others. The lack of significant international treaties for the Euphrates, Tigris, and Jordan rivers will be a significant constraint on optimizing the development and management of these important river basins. Besides questions of water rights and allocations, deterioration in surface water quality due to upstream diversions, depletions, and return flows will become an international issue of increasing importance. Ongoing studies for the Jordan river are being supported by the Bank and other international agencies and may lead to joint programs in the context of the peace negotiations. Similar exercises will be required for other shared rivers and aquifers.

Conclusions

Institutional reform is a central requirement for comprehensive water planning and management, yet is one of the most difficult measures to implement. No standard solutions are possible and reform must reflect the particular country and context. The weakness of many governmental agencies is a matter for serious concern, and is an issue that cannot be bypassed or avoided. The nature of the resource requires that governments set long-term strategies and allocation policies, handle most problems of resource reallocation, and establish and enforce quality standards. Even with respect to the delivery of water services, for which privatization and the increased use of incentive mechanisms are of prime importance, governments are still required to create the planning and regulatory framework within which to promote financial discipline and efficient use in line with underlying economic realities. Since there is little evidence that ad hoc institutional change provides a satisfactory basis for effective management, institutional issues need to be tackled in an integrated and coherent manner as a basis for the implementation of national and international strategies that are further reviewed in the next chapter.

5. Water Strategies for the MENA Region

Strategies at the National Level

Emphasis on individual specific projects and sectors is inherently unsatisfactory under the conditions of water scarcity and growing environmental stress found throughout the region. Arguments in favor of developing an integrated approach to water management are therefore persuasive. Key principles set out in previous chapters, which should guide the formulation of national water strategy, include the following.

- Water resources should be treated as a unitary resource requiring coherent planning for its effective use and management in order to reflect its full economic value.
- Water quality should be considered simultaneously with water quantity.
- Strong data collection systems and timely data processing and dissemination are critical to all aspects of water resources planning, development, and management.
- Clear statements of national water policy are required, and national water resource management plans, supported by appropriate regional and basin plans, should be consistent with the policy.
- Alternative water development strategies should be systematically evaluated, giving full consideration to the balance between supply and demand management practices and measures.
- Stakeholders at each level in the water resource should be consulted and fully participate in decisionmaking and the selection of alternatives.
- Attention should be given to disadvantaged groups who normally have little say in water management and planning, including women, rural communities, and the urban poor, who should be seen as key stakeholders.

54   A STRATEGY FOR MANAGING WATER IN THE MENA REGION

- Reallocation issues—in particular from agriculture to municipal and industrial water supply—should be given particular attention.
- Demand management and water conservation should be promoted through both economic (e.g., financial incentives, market mechanisms) and noneconomic (e.g., regulatory) measures.
- High priority should be given to institutional strengthening of governmental agencies responsible for development of sustainable water sector policies, programs, and infrastructure.
- Delivery of water services should, to the extent possible, be decentralized to financially autonomous utilities, which may be public corporations, private firms, cooperatives, or user groups.
- Privatization of utility services should be promoted, including not only full divestiture of utility companies but also contracting out of services or utility management, "corporatization" of public utilities, BOT arrangements and increased user involvement (e.g., in irrigation).
- Agreements between riparian countries should provide the basis for water allocation and investment activities on international rivers, covering surface water, groundwater, and water quality.

Harmonization of Water Resource and Environmental Objectives

The more traditional water resource issues concerning supply and demand should be supplemented by broad based concern for protecting environmental values associated with natural water conditions. Particular attention should be given to the management of critical ecosystems such as coastal lagoons and inland wetlands. Water policy objectives, instruments, and programs therefore need to reflect environmental concerns; balancing water use for maintaining natural conditions with other competing water uses should be specifically addressed in water policy statements. Policies for protecting natural water environments should be incorporated into water allocation principles and regulatory measures that control water resources development and management.

Financing

Even with a shift away from investments in new supply, water programs can be very costly. Funding must compete with programs in other sectors often under conditions of financial stringency. Major emphasis should therefore be given to developing new sources of funds to supplement the traditional heavy emphasis on national budgetary allocations. Chief among these approaches are measures that seek to mobilize local funds, in particular under the "user pays" and "polluter pays" principles. However, the absence in most countries of the region of modern utilities that meter and charge for their services, coupled with the ineffectiveness of most regulatory controls, will limit the resources that can in practice be so mobilized. Building the necessary institutional capacity and generating support and participation by stakeholders in assuming financial responsibility, although critically important, will be a difficult and time-consuming process. Inevitably, therefore, national funding will remain a primary requirement. Given the acute economic difficulties faced in many MENA countries, this will in turn require continued heavy dependence on foreign sources of assistance. The contribution of the World Bank to water development and conservation efforts, and its role in mobilizing foreign assistance from other sources, will be a significant factor in this equation.

Country Water Assessments and National Strategies

Water planning is a continuous and iterative process, and there is no alternative to a strong permanent institutional capacity to contribute the analytical basis for sound decisionmaking. But preparation of a country water assessment leading to a national water strategy (chapter 1) will often be a vital step to clarify application of the general principles in a specific country, develop a coherent framework, and reach consensus among the many participants in the water sector. Such a country water assessment and strategy would take stock of current and prospective problems and issues and set out a long-term strategy for water resource development and management. As such, it would provide a framework for consistency in sectoral reform efforts and coordination of donor support. It would establish priorities for further analytical work and review the criteria and institutional measures needed to establish planning on a sound basis.

Strategies at the Sectoral Level

Preparing a country water assessment will often require finding solutions to acute and/or emerging water shortages. The answers to meeting these water shortages will lie not only in the approaches to resource management summarized above but also in increased efficiency within specific sectors, in particular agriculture, by far the dominant user. Moreover, the impact of specific sectors on instream uses, such as fisheries and wildlife or recreation, will require increased attention. Similarly, the reuse of treated wastewater to different standards for

56   A STRATEGY FOR MANAGING WATER IN THE MENA REGION

different specific uses will become of increasing significance throughout the region. In this context, and in parallel with renewed attention to certain classical types of interventions (water charges, strengthening institutions, and so on), sector-specific actions and interventions (e.g., reducing unaccounted-for water or introducing drip irrigation) will warrant special attention in future operations.

Apparent water savings to be expected from specific water conservation measures need careful hydrological analysis, as apparent losses from one project may be reused by others downstream. They will also need to be compared with alternatives for saving or mobilizing water, including wastewater reuse. In most cases, however, conservation measures can be expected to be economically viable, in particular where water savings result in production increases, as is often the case where modern irrigation technologies are introduced.

Irrigated Agriculture

Conservation measures to be considered in irrigated agriculture include improved water scheduling and operations; modernization of irrigation networks and onfarm systems, modifications in cropping patterns (e.g., through the use of less water intensive or salt tolerant crops), and adoption of complementary agricultural practices. Such measures need to be supported by appropriate irrigation and agricultural research programs which are themselves attuned to the national water policy.

Improved irrigation scheduling both at the system and farm levels needs to be given high priority to ensure that—within the constraints of system design and management capability—optimum crop water requirements are met with a minimum of water losses while avoiding soil salinization and waterlogging. Such programs often have the potential for significant water savings at relatively low cost. Benefits may be great in advanced irrigation systems, for instance in respect of micro irrigation. For example, in Israel, systematic scheduling of water in response to soil moisture measurements—in association with the adoption of drip irrigation and a range of other measures—has helped reduce field water application rates by more than 40 percent while at the same time productivity has increased.

Inadequate attention has been paid in many MENA countries to the possibilities of upgrading irrigation systems to higher technical standards. Even where advanced conveyance and distribution systems have been adopted (e.g., in Morocco and Tunisia), little has been made of the potential created for upgrading water application methods. Modern irrigation techniques range from improved surface irrigation methods to sprinkler and micro irrigation (drip or trickle). These techniques need to be carefully selected and adapted to the local physical, agronomic, and socioeconomic environment, as well as to the technical and managerial skills of local farmers. This latter point is particularly important; most sophisticated irrigation techniques require substantial onfarm and related investments (onfarm water storage facilities, changes in tertiary and quaternary distribution systems, etc.) besides being dependent on a reliable and predictable water supply. Upgrading existing irrigation systems should in most cases be preceded by pilot schemes to experiment with alternative design concepts. Costly improved technologies can only be justified if their agronomic and economic potential is fully exploited. High priority should therefore be given to systematic research programs for identifying better irrigation practices and more remunerative crops. Moreover, nationwide irrigation research and extension projects need to be promoted in parallel to system modernization and rehabilitation as is being done in Morocco.

Municipal and Industrial Supply

Urban water consumption will rise rapidly in the MENA region owing to population growth, urbanization, industrial development, and per capita income growth. Satisfying demands will be a major challenge. First priority must be given to improved water delivery efficiency and to conservation. Even in countries such as Jordan and Algeria that face acute water shortages and despite numerous attempts to correct deficiencies unaccounted-for-water can still reach unacceptable levels of more than 50 percent. An important consequence of reducing municipal water use is that it results in reductions in the volume of wastewater discharged for collection, treatment, and disposal. A range of institutional, technological, and administrative measures will be required at the national, local, and enterprise levels to rationalize water consumption. These should include policy reforms in setting charges for water use and wastewater disposal, implementation of effective metering and billing systems, water conservation studies, investment in major facilities and distribution networks to reduce waste (leakage control), and public education programs.

Most industrial water is used for disposing of heat or other waste, and is returned to the stream, little water is actually consumed by industry so that industrial use of water primarily affects water quality. In all MENA countries, the costs of alternative industrial processes that can produce the same output while using less water and fewer adverse consequences for water quality should always be examined. Internal recycling is a primary alternative. Recycling of water for process uses—such as washing or the transport of dissolved materials—is generally more expensive than for cooling, although the costs of water supply and wastewater disposal for industry are typically less than 2 percent of production costs. Location of industry and zoning laws should be given major importance since concentration of wastes in one area can simplify treatment and minimize the adverse effects on other users. Environmental impact assessments and locally adapted water prices would contribute to better siting of new industrial plants.

Thermal power plants raise particular issues. Demands for electrical energy in MENA countries will continue to grow rapidly with industrialization and income growth. Such demands will be met in large part by the construction of thermal plants. Many of these plants will exceed 1000 megawatts (MW) in size. Although generally more efficient and economical than smaller plants, large plants heighten the potential waste heat problem, raising the possibility that some local waters will not be able to support the increased consumptive losses or assimilate the heat without auxiliary cooling facilities. Water resources planning studies should be broadened to include greater consideration of sites for thermal electric power generation and their possible effects on water resources. Alternative options to the use of freshwater should also be considered (e.g., the use of seawater or the adoption of air cooling techniques).

Rural Water Supply

Rural water supply seldom makes major demands on the local water resource although it can be relatively costly, and numerous, widely dispersed schemes are often difficult to manage and maintain. Nevertheless, in poorer countries with inadequate coverage, rural water supply can be a principle means of improving health standards. Appropriate technologies are required together with innovative programs to transfer management to local groups with government technical and related support provided as necessary. Sewerage services are seldom justified in rural areas, although the design of water supply systems must critically take into account the location of pollution sources.

Wastewater Treatment and Use

Treatment of wastewater will become a major burden on MENA countries. Measures to decrease municipal and industrial water use would lead to reductions in the amount of wastewater and, consequently, also to reductions in the size and costs of collectors, treatment plants, and disposal systems. A critical problem in the development and implementation of effective municipal wastewater management is the practice—common to most MENA countries—of having industrial plants discharge their wastewaters, generally with little or no pretreatment, into the municipal wastewater systems. Pretreatment of industrial wastewater is often crucial so that biological treatment processes can operate efficiently.

Plans for using treated wastewater as a source of water supply in water-short areas should receive attention. Such plans should consider all alternative uses of wastewater including in particular in irrigation and for combatting seawater intrusion. Irrigation of green spaces in urban areas is another possibility although the health risks associated with such programs should be recognized. Reuse programs may be either directly or indirectly related to groundwater recharge schemes. Due attention should be given to institutional, environmental, and health aspects and issues of cost sharing and water charges. The agrosanitation concept developed in Israel under which a city government and adjacent farmers reached legally binding agreements and shared costs may have application elsewhere in the region. Many governments, however, have not dealt with these aspects of wastewater and considerable lead time may be required to find satisfactory solutions. But for economic and environmental reasons solutions must be found

Instream Effects

Water quality protection is an increasingly important component of water resources management in MENA countries. The potential danger to potable aquifers, in particular, should not be underestimated. In tackling these issues, a strong planning and regulatory framework is indispensable. Effective water quality protection requires programs for each of the multiple sources of water pollution: municipal and industrial point source effluent discharges into surface waters; waste storage and disposal systems with potential for polluting surface and groundwater, land development and land use activities (primarily agricultural) serving as nonpoint sources of pollution, and water project operations that alter water quality. Coordination among control programs addressing different sources of pollution is important to ensure the best use of limited financial resources.

The natural potential for flash flood damage in the region has been substantially reduced by engineering works—including storage reservoirs, levees, channel improvements and bypasses—built in the last few decades. There is, however, a need to change the way countries perceive

60   A STRATEGY FOR MANAGING WATER IN THE MENA REGION

their flood problems. In general, the cumulative value of a river's flood pulse—nutrient supply to floodplains, natural floodwater irrigation, groundwater recharge, fisheries, and so on—has with few exceptions been underestimated. Long-term economic interests may be better served by building on the flood pulse, promoting locally flood-dependent production systems—recessional agriculture, floodplain fisheries, and grazing—rather than suppressing them. In the predominantly arid MENA region, relying on the flood-pulse, or indeed mimicking the flood pulse by releases from storage reservoirs, is also more compatible with biodiversity maintenance and traditional local controls of water. Broadly conceived and planned watershed programs are often preferable to the construction of a few large reservoirs; and experience worldwide has shown that balanced development has been undermined by uncontrolled private exploitation of water resources.

In some MENA countries, hydropower accounts for a substantial portion of the total electric energy generated. Although hydropower generation does not consume water, it may have an impact on the timing of flows within the water resource system. Moreover, the location of diversion points for nonpower uses may affect electric generation potentials and thereby the potential total value of water use in the system. Power projects need therefore to be closely planned in association with overall river management.

Large rivers such as the Nile, Tigris, and Euphrates are used for navigation with little or no effect upon water. But in some cases, substantial regulation of flows is required to facilitate navigation; this can have significant effects in the low-flow season and in smaller rivers. The value of water for navigation—the difference between economic costs of water transport and those of the least-cost alternative mode of transportation—should always be examined. On major waterways, water can often be expected to have a positive value for navigation. However, for smaller waterways, the benefits may be insufficient to cover the costs of constructing and operating transport facilities.

World Bank Strategy at the National Level

Staff in the MENA region will aim to implement the approved Bank policy. Previous chapters have suggested guiding principles. With respect to individual countries, Bank staff will review and clarify water resource objectives on a country-by-country basis and schedule Bank activities to meet those objectives. Countries will be encouraged to prepare country water assessments as an appropriate instrument for assessing the present state of water resources planning and management, guiding the preparation of a country strategy, and preparing a framework for Bank and other donors both in the water sector as a whole and in individual water-using subsectors. Depending on the issues, and on the state of preparedness, such assessments could in principle lead directly to Bank lending.

The Lending Program

Program and project lending instruments will be developed to promote agreed water development objectives supported by appropriate economic and sector work and technical assistance. An essential feature of such broad-based lending activities is that they will deal with the water sector in an holistic manner, and will be designed to promote an integrated approach to water resources management. The overriding objective will be to avoid fragmented development and the wasteful use of the scarce resource. But individual sectors face issues that go beyond those typically associated with resource management, for instance municipal finance in relation to water supply and sanitation, or agricultural policy and reform in relation to irrigation. These issues in their nature cannot be tackled satisfactorily in the context of broad-based operations. Typically, therefore, the Bank will promote a program of complementary lending at the level both of the resource and of individual sectors, with all the individual operations framed within the context of an overall strategy for water resources.

Some countries may be unsuited to a broad based water resources management operation, or unwilling to accept the concept. Multipurpose and single-purpose investment projects may still be justified. Other options could include lending for high-priority cross-sectoral activities (for instance, in support of data systems, dam safety improvement or O&M programs), and environmental initiatives could complement water resources approaches focusing in particular on the regulatory function. With or without broad-based water resources operations, however, all such projects will need to be framed and prioritized within appropriate national, regional, and basin plans and be designed to assure consistency with overall country water strategy and water resources objectives.

Sector Work and Technical Assistance

Implications for the Bank's sector work and technical assistance are straightforward. Priority in water operations will be given to assisting countries in the preparation of country water assessments and water strategy documents. The water strategy would itself schedule further

62   A STRATEGY FOR MANAGING WATER IN THE MENA REGION

detailed planning and other studies and determine which of these would require additional Bank involvement or technical assistance support. In the case where major water resource planning assistance is required, donors would be encouraged to support the essential work with grant funds wherever feasible. The Bank could act as executing agency. Similarly, as preparation of the country water assessment could lead directly to priority lending, project preparation facility funding might be applicable.

Particular attention will also be given to coordinating environmental work with the issues relating to water resources development and management. While the focus of an environmental action plan or impact assessment differs from that of a country water assessment or a river-basin plan, there is nevertheless considerable interaction between the two. Water often represents the critical environmental issue in arid regions, and recommendations in the context of environmental sector work must be realistic and practical in regard to resource management issues. Similarly, issues of water quality are inherent to any water strategy; country water assessments and other water sector work must therefore reflect environmental concerns in an integral manner.

World Bank Strategy at the International Level

The prominence of international rivers and aquifers in the MENA region limits the extent to which water problems can be resolved solely at the country level, though a carefully documented assessment of its own water resources and objectives is clearly required before a country enters into an international planning exercise and related negotiations. Reaching agreement on international waters is a time consuming and complex process. In MENA, such a process is particularly difficult given that acute conflicts over water are exacerbated by the political sensitivity of relationships between riparian countries. Cooperation often depends on exploiting windows of opportunity. The recent flurry of diplomatic activity by riparian countries on the Jordan river, and the studies initiated with Bank assistance in the context of the Middle East Peace Initiative, may represent such an opportunity.

Each international river basin is unique and no common strategy can be proposed. Nevertheless, experience worldwide has consistently shown that the use of third parties in a mediation role can facilitate dispute resolution, guide complex bargaining towards acceptable outcomes, and help maintain balance and commitment by riparians to the negotiating process. The Bank has many advantages as such a third party since it can (1) act as independent broker; (2) provide leadership inherent in its international role in donor coordination; (3) catalyze the mobilization of both official and private funding; (4) provide an important channel for gaining access to expertise; (5) be creative in promoting appropriate process solutions; and (6) help ensure systematic evaluation of alternative solutions through the appropriate use of analytical techniques.

The Bank has long recognized both the opportunities and risks of such a mediation role. Its contribution to the Indus agreement was perhaps its most notable success in promoting international water agreement. It has also played an active role in respect of the Orange and Komati rivers in Southern Africa. Whether a successful role can be developed in MENA remains to be seen although its involvement in the Jordan basin already shows promise. While recognizing that involvement must be at the request of the riparians, provided this is forthcoming, the Bank's recently approved policy proposes a more pro-active role, covering not only surface waters but also possibly joint management of shared groundwater resources.

Concluding Remarks

Water resource problems in MENA are among the most urgent, complex, and intractable of any region in the world. And though any strategy must be flexible and tailored to the requirements of individual countries and river basins, there are elements that are common to any effective process. These have been delineated in this chapter and the potential role of the Bank in their support has been briefly discussed. Several governments have demonstrated their commitment to tackling water issues in a coordinated and comprehensive manner and, for example, Morocco and Tunisia have both launched initiatives to prepare a country water assessment on which they are likely to base their water investment programs. The World Bank can add impetus to such initiatives and stands ready to provide technical, financial, legal and intermediary support in the context both of individual countries and of international river basins where a consensus of the riparian countries can be reached that this would be helpful.

Appendix Tables

Table A-1. Projects with Water as Primary Purpose, by Region,
FY 1960–Mid-FY 1992
(US$ millions)

Region	Irrigation and drainage		Water supply and sanitation		Hydro-power		Total water		Total lending	
	No.	Amt.	No.	Amt.	No.	Amt.	No.	Amt.	No.	Amt.
Africa	54	966	72	2,042	25	759	151	3,767	1,770	42,085
EAP	78	4,574	37	2,017	15	1,101	130	7,692	892	58,289
ECA	27	1,501	18	1,072	14	848	59	3,421	373	29,463
LAC	39	2,724	67	3,893	61	3,088	167	9,705	1,126	72,965
SAS	112	6,584	35	1,742	13	2,415	160	10,741	797	57,466
Past borrowers[a]	5	139	7	97	5	93	17	329	136	3,464
MENA	43	1,616	51	2,084	4	230	98	3,930	548	23,134
Total	358	18,104	287	12,947	137	8,534	782	39,585	5,642	286,866

a. Past borrowers to which the World Bank no longer lends.
Source: World Bank data.

66 A STRATEGY FOR MANAGING WATER IN THE MENA REGION

Table A-2. Projects with Water as Primary Purpose in MENA,
FY 1960-Mid-FY 1992
(US$ millions)

Region	Irrigation and drainage		Water supply and sanitation		Hydro-power		Total water		Total lending	
	No.	Amt.	No.	Amt.	No.	Amt.	No.	Amt.	No.	Amt.
Algeria	5	283	5	889	0	0	10	1,172	50	4,170
Egypt	10	589	5	155	0	0	15	744	84	5,008
Iran	2	52	0	0	0	0	2	52	34	1,448
Iraq	1	40	0	0	0	0	1	40	5	143
Jordan	1	8	8	155	0	0	9	163	48	1,128
Morocco	9	296	6	305	4	230	19	831	98	6,179
Oman	0	0	0	0	0	0	0	0	11	157
Syria	2	103	5	200	0	0	7	303	21	661
Tunisia	6	151	11	289	0	0	17	440	95	3,133
Yemen	7	95	11	91	0	0	18	186	98	1,009
Total	43	1,617	51	2,084	4	230	98	3,931	544	23,036

Note: Figures are based on loans/credits approved by the Board between 1960 and mid-FY 1992 and do not reflect cancellations.

Source: World Bank data.

APPENDIX A   67

*Table A-3. Sector Studies and Memoranda with Water Component,
MENA Region*

Country	Date	Title
Algeria	1981	Irrigation Sector Review
	1990	Agriculture: Opportunity for Growth
	1991	Water Supply Sector Strategy
	1992	Water Sector Review (draft)
Egypt	1981	Irrigation and Land Reclamation Review
	1982	Electric Power Subsector Study
	1982	Agriculture Sector Memorandum
	1983	Greater Cairo Sector Memorandum
	1984	Water Supply and Sewerage Review
	1985	Power Generation Investment Review
	1986	Issues in Agriculture Strategy
	1990	Land Reclamation Subsector Study
	1992	Water and Wastewater Review (draft)
	1992	Environmental Action Plan (draft)
Iran	1992	Agriculture Sector Note
Jordan	1981	Rainfed Agriculture Subsector Study
	1983	Urban Sector Review
	1984	Water Supply and Sewerage Memorandum
	1984	Water Sector Study
	1988	Water Resources Sector Study
	1990	Agriculture Sector Strategy Review
Morocco	1980	Agriculture Sector: Issues and Strategy
	1980	Water Supply and Sewerage Review
	1982	Urban Sector Review and Project Identification
	1984	Power Subsector Study
	Proposed	Irrigation and Water Sector Review
Syria	1986	Water Supply and Sewerage Sector Memo.
	1987	Agriculture Sector Survey
Tunisia	1980	Irrigation Subsector Memorandum
	1981	Agriculture Sector Memorandum
	1982	Agriculture Sector Survey
	Proposed	Water Efficiency Study
Yemen	1973	Water Supply and Sewerage Study
	1981	Urban Sector Memorandum
	1983	Water Supply and Sanitation
	1983	Agriculture Sector Memorandum
	1988	Renewable Resource Management Review
	1989	Irrigation Sector Study
	1992	Agriculture Sector Study
	Proposed	Environmental Action Plan

Source: World Bank data. Reports are available from the World Bank Information
Center.

68 A STRATEGY FOR MANAGING WATER IN THE MENA REGION

Table A-4.   Water Availabilty, MENA Region

Country	Total annual internal renewable water resources BCM	Annual river flows		Net annual renewable resources BCM	Renewable resources per capita		
		From other countries BCM	To other countries BCM		1960	1990	2025
					Cubic meters per year		
Algeria	18.90	0.20	0.70	18.40	1,704	737	354
Bahrain	n.a.	n.a.	n.a.	n.a.	n.a.	n.a.	n.a.
Egypt	1.80	56.50	(**)	58.30	2,251	1,112	645
Iran	117.50	(**)	(**)	117.50	5,788	2,152	1,032
Iraq	34.00	66.00	n.a.	100.00	14,706	5,285	2,000
Israel	1.70	0.45	n.a.	2.15	1,024	467	311
Jordan	0.70	0.16	(**)	0.86	529	224	91
Lebanon	4.80	n.a.	0.86	3.94	2,000	1,407	809
Libya	0.70	n.a.	n.a.	0.70	538	154	55
Malta	n.a.	n.a.	n.a.	n.a.	100	75	75
Morocco	30.00	n.a.	0.30	29.70	2,560	1,185	651
Oman	2.00	n.a.	(**)	2.00	4,000	1,333	421
Qatar	n.a.	n.a.	(**)	0.00	n.a.	n.a.	n.a.
Saudi Arabia	2.20	n.a.	(**)	2.20	537	156	49
Syria	7.60	27.90	30.00	5.50	1,196	439	161
Tunisia	3.75	0.60	n.a.	4.35	1,036	532	319
UAE	0.30	n.a.	n.a.	0.30	3,000	189	113
Yemen	2.50	n.a.	(**)	2.50	481	214	72
MENA	228.45	152.05	31.86	348.64	3,430	1,436	667
Africa	4,184.00	n.a.	n.a.	4,184.00	14,884	6,516	2,620
Asia	10,485.00	(**)	(**)	10,485.00	6,290	3,368	2,134
World	40,673.00	n.a.	n.a.	40,673.00	13,471	7,685	4,783

(**) Cross border flows not known but assumed insignificant.
n.a. Not available.
Source: World Resources Institute 1991–92 and 1992–93, and World Bank estimates.

APPENDIX A   69

Table A-5. Water Withdrawal, MENA Region

Country	Net annual internal renewable resources BCM	Year of data	Total annual withdrawal BCM	Percent of water resource	Proportion of withdrawals per sector Domestic	Industry	Agriculture
					(Percent of total withdrawal)		
Algeria	18.40	1980	3.0	16	22	4	74
Bahrain	n.a.	1975	0.2	n.a.	60	36	4
Egypt	58.30	1985	56.4	97	7	5	88
Iran	117.50	1975	45.4	39	4	9	87
Iraq	100.00	1970	42.8	43	3	5	92
Israel	2.15	1986	1.9	88	16	5	79
Jordan	0.90	1987	0.8	87	29	6	65
Lebanon	3.80	1975	0.8	16	11	4	85
Libya	0.70	1985	2.8	404	15	10	75
Malta	n.a.	1978	n.a.	92	76	8	16
Morocco	29.70	1985	11.0	37	6	3	91
Oman	2.00	1975	0.4	22	3	3	94
Qatar	0.00	1975	n.a.	174	36	26	38
Saudi Arabia	2.20	1975	2.3	106	45	51	4
Syria	5.50	1976	3.3	61	7	10	83
Tunisia	4.35	1985	2.3	53	13	7	80
UAE	0.30	1980	0.4	140	11	9	80
Yemen	2.50	1987	3.4	136	5	2	93
MENA	348.30		177.2	51	6	7	87
Africa	4,184.00		144.0	3	7	5	88
Asia	10,485.00		1,531.0	15	6	8	86
World	40,673.00		3,240.0	8	8	23	69

n.a. Not available.
Source: World Resources Institute 1991–92 and 1992–93, and World Bank estimates.

70 A STRATEGY FOR MANAGING WATER IN THE MENA REGION

Table A-6. Irrigated Areas, MENA Region

	1970			1987		
	Area cultivated ('000 hectares)	Area irrigated ('000 hectares)	Irrigated as percent of area cultivated	Area cultivated ('000 hectares)	Area irrigated ('000 hectares)	Irrigated as percent of area cultivated
Algeria	6,800	238	3.5	7,540	360	4.8
Bahrain	2	1	50.0	2	1	50.0
Egypt	2,843	2,843	100.0	2,571	2,571	100.0
Iran	15,700	5,200	33.1	14,830	5,740	38.7
Iraq	4,993	1,480	29.6	5,450	1,750	32.1
Israel	409	168	41.1	433	278	64.2
Jordan	314	34	10.8	374	46	12.3
Lebanon	325	68	20.9	301	86	28.6
Libya	2,025	175	8.6	2,145	238	11.1
Malta	n.a.	n.a.	n.a.	n.a.	n.a.	n.a.
Morocco	7,505	920	12.3	8,731	1,255	14.4
Oman	32	29	90.6	48	41	85.4
Qatar	3	2	66.7	5	3	60.0
Saudi Arabia	870	365	42.0	1,185	425	35.9
Syria	5,909	451	7.6	5,560	654	11.8
Tunisia	4,480	90	2.0	4,811	270	5.6
UAE	12	5	41.7	39	5	12.8
Yemen	1,140	260	22.8	1,338	320	23.9
MENA	53,362	12,329	23.1	55,363	14,043	25.4
Africa	145,073	4,593	3.2	159,733	6,363	4.0
Asia	375,372	97,430	26.0	387,668	128,086	33.0
World	1,445,364	168,575	11.7	1,477,877	227,108	15.4

n.a. Not available.

Source: United States Department of Agriculture (USDA) 1993.

References

Bhatia Ramesh, Rita Cesti, and James Winpenny. 1993. *Policies for water conservation and reallocation: good practice cases in improving efficiency and equity.* Technical Paper No. ___. World Bank, Washington, D.C.

Burchi S. 1989. *Current Developments and Trends in Water Resources Legislation and Administration.* Paper for the third conference on the International Association of Water Law. Alicante.

Coopers & Lybrand. 1993. *Institutional Framework for Effective Water Resources Management in the Middle East and North Africa.* Report prepared for the Mediterranean Environmental Technical Assistance Program (METAP). London.

Frederick, K. D. 1993. *Balancing Eater Demands with Supplies: The Role of Demand Management in a World of Increasing Scarcity.* Technical Paper 189, World Bank, Washington, D.C.

Operations Evaluation Department. 1981. *Water Management Study of Twenty Six Audits of Bank-assisted Irrigation Projects.* World Bank, Washington, D.C.

_____. 1991. *Review of Twenty One Impact Evaluation Studies of Irrigation projects between 1979 and 1990.* World Bank, Washington, D.C.

_____. 1992. *Water Supply and Sanitation Projects: the Bank's Experience, 1967–1989.* World Bank, Washington, D.C.

Rogers, Peter. 1992. "Comprehensive Water Resource Management: A Concept Paper." Working Paper Series 879. Infrastructure and Urban Development Department. World Bank, Washington, D.C.

United Nations. 1991. *A Strategy for Water Sector Capacity Building.* Proceedings of a United Nations Development Program (UNDP) Symposium. Delft.

United Nations Environmental Program. 1992. *Final Report of the International Conference on Water and the Environment.* Dublin.

United Nations Department of Technical Cooperation. 1991, *Demand Management: A Strategy for the Implementation of the Mar del Plata Plan for the 1990s.* United Nations, New York.

van Tuijl, Willem. 1992. *Improving Water Use Efficiency in Agriculture: Experiences in the Middle East and North Africa.* Technical Paper No. 201. World Bank. Washington D.C.

World Bank. 1993a. *Water Resources Management: A Policy Paper.* Washington, D.C.

———. 1993b. *Water Sector Strategies: a Guide.* Draft. Washington, D.C.

World Resources Institute, in collaboration with the United Nations Environment Programme and the United Nations Development Programme. 1992. *World Resources 1992–93.* Oxford University Press. New York.